Ten Steps to Fundraising Success

Ten Steps to Fundraising Success

Choosing the Right
Strategy for Your
Organization

Mal Warwick
Stephen Hitchcock

JOSSEY-BASS
A Wiley Company
www.josseybass.com

JOSSEY-BASS
A Wiley Company
989 Market Street
San Francisco, CA 94103-1741

www.josseybass.com

Library of Congress Cataloging-in-Publication Data
Warwick, Mal.
    Ten steps to fundraising success: choosing the right strategy for your organization /
Mal Warwick, Stephen Hitchcock.—1st ed.
        p. cm.—(The Jossey-Bass Nonprofit and public management series)
    ISBN 0–7879–5674–0 (alk. paper)
    1. Fund raising—United States. 2. Nonprofit organizations—United States—Finance.
I. Hitchcock, Stephen. II. Title. III. Series.
HV41.2 .W47 2002
658.15′224—dc21   2001003769

PB Printing   10 9 8 7 6 5 4 3 2 1   FIRST EDITION

The Jossey-Bass
Nonprofit and Public Management Series

Contents

Figure, Tables, and Exercises

Figure

Tables

Exercises

Acknowledgments

IN THE COURSE of working together for more than fifteen years, we have met with hundreds of nonprofit organizations and participated in dozens of professional conferences. We've come to realize that there are a lot more people who *know* about fundraising than actually *do* it. It's much easier to talk about elaborate theories and intriguing innovations than to get down to the mundane work of asking for charitable gifts, promptly thanking those who make them, and keeping accurate records of those contributions. To succeed in fundraising, you have to genuinely like donors, respect your coworkers, and keep your wits about you as you thread your way through a maze of detail-laden tasks requiring hands-on attention.

All of this is to say that writing a practical workbook turned out to be much more challenging and time-consuming than either of us thought when we blithely agreed to our publisher's suggestion about creating a manual to accompany Mal Warwick's *The Five Strategies for Fundraising Success* (Jossey-Bass, 2000). So we acknowledge with gratitude and respect the multiple contributions of our editors, Dorothy Hearst and Johanna Vondeling. Dorothy's work was central to the success of *The Five Strategies*. And Johanna's patient encouragement and insightful guidance helped transform our collected observations and detailed exercises into a reader-friendly workbook.

This book owes a big debt to *The Five Strategies*. Specifically, the overview of the five strategies in Step Four and the exercises and table in Step Five are from this book. And Tables 8.1 through 8.5 in Step Eight are adapted from Table 14.10 in the book. Several years ago, the authors collaborated in writing *The Hands-On Guide to Fundraising Strategy and Evaluation* (1995; now out of print). The exercises in Steps One, Two, and Eight are adapted from that book.

In a real sense, dozens of dedicated staff from many organizations are the coauthors of this workbook. We are grateful for their gracious collaboration, especially on the part of those who are current clients of Mal Warwick & Associates. Month after month, each of us has the privilege to meet with some of the nation's most outstanding nonprofit groups. Over the years, these informal meetings have evolved into a more formal and structured planning and review process much like that described in this workbook. Although there are rumors that these sessions have occasioned an increase in sick days in the nonprofit sector, there is strong evidence that this process is producing real results.

We are able to spend so much time meeting with clients because we have been blessed with extraordinarily competent and diligent coworkers at Mal Warwick & Associates. We watch with amazement—and learn so much ourselves—as our colleagues manage the finances, data processing, copywriting, graphic design, and all the other aspects of producing mailings and other projects that benefit our clients.

We have dedicated this book to our parents, Harry and Jeanette Warshawsky, and Cliff and Delores Hitchcock. For both of us, they were our first instructors in effective planning and compassionate philanthropy. They coached and challenged us as we took our first steps in serving others. From them, we learned that true success comes from having a mission in life.

About the Authors

Mal Warwick, a consultant, author, and public speaker, has been involved in the not-for-profit sector for nearly forty years. Collectively, he and his associates are responsible for raising at least half a billion dollars, largely in the form of small gifts from individuals. Warwick is the founder and chairman of Mal Warwick & Associates, a fundraising and marketing agency that has served nonprofit organizations since 1979, and of Response Management Technologies, a data processing form for nonprofit organizations. He is also cofounder (with Nick Allen) of donordigital.com LLC, which assists nonprofit organizations on-line, and is a cofounder of Share Group, the nation's leading telephone fundraising firm.

He has written or edited twelve books of interest to nonprofit managers, including *The Five Strategies for Fundraising Success* (Jossey-Bass, 2000) and the standard texts, *Raising Money by Mail* and *How to Write Successful Fundraising Letters* (Jossey-Bass, 2001). He is editor of *Mal Warwick's Newsletter: Successful Direct Mail, Telephone and Online Fundraising,* and is a popular speaker and workshop leader.

He is an active member of the Association of Fundraising Professionals and U.S. country representative of the Resource Alliance, organizers of the annual International Fund Raising Congress; and he served for ten years on the board of the Association of Direct Response Fundraising Counsel, two of those years as president.

Stephen Hitchcock is president of Mal Warwick & Associates, where he has worked since 1986. Among the clients he works with are Bread for the World, a citizens' lobby for hunger in Washington, D.C.; the International Center's New Forests Project; the Pacific School of Religion; the Center for the Victims of Torture; and TreePeople, an environmental and educational organization in Los Angeles.

Hitchcock has conducted workshops for regional and national conferences of the National Society of Fund Raising Executives. He has also taught seminars and workshops sponsored by the Public Broadcasting Service, Trust for Public Land, American Cancer Society, and Planned Parenthood.

Hitchcock's columns appear regularly in *Contributions*, and he is a columnist and contributing editor for the newsletter *Successful Direct Mail and Telephone Fundraising*. He is the coauthor of *The Hands-On Guide to Fundraising Strategy and Evaluation*. He was executive editor of *Corporate 500: The Directory of Corporate Philanthropy* and author of "Fundraising: The Board Is Key" in *The Nonprofit Board Book: Strategies for Organizational Success*.

Introduction

Before You Take Your First Step

DON'T SKIP this introduction. *It includes some of our best ideas and offers useful instructions.*

If somebody is talking about fundraising but not mentioning money, then it's not really fundraising. But if money is all they're talking about, then it's not fundraising either.

Fundraising is not just about money. It's best understood from a broader perspective as resource development. Approached from that vantage point, fundraising is about securing the resources you need—at the right time and the right place—to achieve your organization's *mission*.

The premise that informs this workbook is that simply raising the most money or having the lowest possible percentage of fundraising costs is not necessarily successful fundraising. Even the more sophisticated criterion for success—net contributed income—is an inadequate yardstick for evaluating development programs. Rather, you will be most successful if you select a fundraising strategy that complements your organization's mission. That way, you will do more than just raise the funds your organization needs to meet its immediate financial requirements. You'll also reinforce and help to implement your organization's mission.

Ideally, to take full advantage of this workbook, your institution will have at least some rudiments of a strategic plan. We assume there is a clear articulation of your mission and your overall strategic direction, as well as some delineation of your organization's major goals. If that's not the case, you don't need to stop reading. But you'll derive the most benefit if your organization has a strategic plan. The purpose of this workbook is to help you select a strategy that complements and helps implement your organization's mission as expressed in its overall strategy.

We believe there are five fundamental fundraising strategies that constitute the core of all resource development efforts: Growth, Involvement, Visibility, Efficiency, and Stability (GIVES). Mal Warwick's *The Five Strategies for Fundraising Success* (Jossey-Bass, 2000) makes the case for using these five strategies in a planning process that enables a nonprofit organization to analyze and then strengthen its fundraising program.

This workbook will help you put the GIVES Model to work for your organization. In the following pages, we guide you step by step through this process. This will require that you select one of the five strategies in the GIVES Model as your primary fundraising strategy during the current phase of your organization's history and be single-minded in sticking with that strategy even if other attractive opportunities beckon.

Strategic planning experts routinely say that no strategic plan is useful forever. In fact, most such specialists advise that an organization reassess its strategic plan every three to five years to come to grips with changed circumstances. So it is with fundraising strategy too.

Rarely can any organization thrive indefinitely by pursuing the same fundraising strategy. At some point in its history, your organization almost certainly must change the way it goes about its resource development activities. The natural evolution of fundraising techniques, the impact of external events, and the logic of organizational development make it imperative for your organization to reevaluate its fundraising strategy every several years. And if you haven't yet done that even once, time's a-wasting!

This workbook is designed to (1) guide the process of selecting the best fundraising strategy for your organization or (2) help you undertake the periodic reevaluation of your group's development strategy. The exercises will guide your personal reflection, and you can use them to facilitate the discussion process that we believe will help you select the strategy that will lead to fundraising success.

Who Should Use This Workbook, and Why

There are three kinds of people in fundraising:

1. People who are new to fundraising and haven't yet figured out how rich and diverse, and how downright confusing, the field can be

2. People who have been around long enough to know how much they don't understand

3. People who have been in the field seemingly forever and know more about fundraising than just about anyone they ever have to deal with

We suggest that you can benefit from using this workbook regardless of the category you fall into:

- *If your knowledge is limited.* Whether you are a neophyte development staff person, a volunteer, a member of the board of trustees, a committed donor, or a nonprofit executive with broader responsibilities, *Ten Steps to Fundraising Success* can help you make your way, step by step, through the thickets of the fundraising forest. By completing the simple exercises, you should come out of this process with a big-picture understanding of the dynamics of the fundraising process as it applies to the unique circumstances of your organization.
- *If you've already got a good grasp of fundraising fundamentals.* If you're deeply involved in the day-to-day work of resource development for your organization, you'll find this workbook a useful tool to evaluate your fundraising efforts and plot a new course that can help you claim greater rewards for your organization.
- *If you're an old hand at fundraising.* If you think you've seen it all, you may be right! But *Ten Steps to Fundraising Success* will help you see the fundraising process and your own efforts in the field in an entirely new light. The fresh perspective laid out in this workbook will help you reassess what you've done in the past and weigh your course for the future, and the strategic planning process set out in these pages will help you work in a productive and congenial environment with other key people in your organization. As you follow this process, you'll discover lots of opportunities to involve and train others and to increase mutual understanding.

Ten Steps to Fundraising Success is based on *The Five Strategies for Fundraising Success.* If you've read that book, using this workbook should be a snap. But even if you haven't read it, you won't encounter any difficulty following this workbook.

This book is not an exposition of the five strategies, but rather a workbook that uses the five-strategy framework. In a sense, our goal here is both larger and more practical: to provide a process that will help you create a multifaceted fundraising plan that complements your organization's mission. We have written *Ten Steps to Fundraising Success* to stand alone, and we hope you'll find it easy to read, easy to use, and, most important, useful, regardless of your circumstances.

How to Use This Workbook

There are three very good ways to use this workbook:

1. Reading it by yourself cover to cover

2. Using one or more chapters or sets of exercises to address some specific issue that your organization faces

3. Following the entire planning process we set out

Each author of this workbook has served for more than two decades as a consultant to nonprofit organizations. We have had the good fortune to work with hundreds of groups, small, medium, and large, all over the country and across the spectrum of charitable endeavor. Our experience is that everyone and anyone in an organization can make a difference, regardless of job title or formal authority. Because Americans are philanthropic and because they care about the organizations they support, they will respond to almost any new or streamlined giving opportunity that a nonprofit organization incorporates into its fundraising program.

So if you're just one person by yourself, you will benefit from this workbook. Each step will take you about twenty to thirty minutes to read all the way through. Thus, if you spend only three to four hours reading this book and responding to as many of the exercises as possible, you'll have a much better overview of nonprofit fundraising—along with dozens of new ideas to consider for your work.

You may find it helpful to use just parts of this workbook. Your organization's fundraising program may be in good shape and producing the revenue you need, but there are one or two specific problems you want to solve. Or perhaps you're considering undertaking a new initiative like a special event or a planned giving program. You'll find individual exercises to help you evaluate your course of action. In most cases, the individual steps and each of the exercises stand on their own.

We hope, though, that some readers will use the book in the third way: by following the entire process, step by step. You don't need to respond to every question or fill out every exercise. But if you can assemble a team of people and devote at least some time to every step, your organization's fundraising will be strengthened significantly.

Strategic planning is not a fruitful exercise for a lone individual. It's most effective when key stakeholders in an organization fully buy into the process. And that's just as true in setting fundraising strategy as it is in any other critical area of your organization's operations.

Without broad-based consent, it's highly unlikely that you will be able to make the difficult choices involved in concentrating your development activities around one core strategic concept. If you determine your fundraising strategy through a deliberate discussion that involves your board of directors, key volunteers, and responsible staff, then it will be much easier to implement that strategy—and your chances of success will be much higher.

If you decide to assemble a team of key individuals and follow the entire process, we encourage you to avoid spending too much time in planning. The point of all this is to raise more money for your organization, not to create the perfect plan. You could devote dozens of meetings and months of work to crafting and reviewing plans. We instead urge you to limit yourself to three to six meetings of two to three hours each (or one or two weekend retreats). The initial ideas and immediate responses to the exercises we've created will, in most instances, produce more than adequate information and lots of useful insights. From this admittedly incomplete data, we're confident you can select the best strategy for your organization's fundraising success.

What's Ahead

This workbook is organized into ten chapters that correspond to the ten steps we've set out. We've tried to construct this book to help you move, step by step, through the process of applying the GIVES Model to your organization:

Step One: We help you assess your organization's current fundraising efforts. Using a series of four exercises, you will zero in on the most critical elements that lead to success or failure in resource development.

Step Two: The exercises in this step continue the assessment process by helping you evaluate board members, executive staff, and development personnel. You'll discover the skills and experience levels of those who will play key roles in implementing your new fundraising strategy.

Step Three: In this chapter, we help you assemble a team to select the best strategy for your organization, offer suggestions for creating an environment conducive to discussion, and provide a tentative outline for organizing your fundraising planning sessions.

Step Four: You'll gain an overview of the GIVES Model, and you'll weigh the costs and benefits of each of the five strategies for fundraising success in the light of your organization's unique mission and circumstances.

Step Five: Two comprehensive exercises will help guide you and your colleagues through the process of choosing the right combination of primary and secondary fundraising strategies to set a course in resource development that's uniquely appropriate for your organization.

Step Six: A systematic process with five exercises will help you set appropriate fundraising goals consistent with the strategy you've chosen.

Step Seven: A simple exercise, repeated as often as necessary, will allow you to turn your fundraising goals into achievable objectives.

Step Eight: You'll gain an overview of the potential applications of the ten most common fundraising techniques, with in-depth exploration of the five most widely used of these techniques.

Step Nine: You'll find a useful tool that will help you stay on schedule and deploy the resources you need when you most need them, even though you don't have all the answers.

Step Ten: Five simple exercises will help you measure your organization's progress in achieving its fundraising objectives and goal—and help you see what areas deserve further review and remedial attention.

We've prepared a simple chart (Figure I.1) to illustrate the cyclical nature of the planning process in this workbook. Along the way (at least every six

FIGURE I.1

The Ten-Step Planning Process for Fundraising Success

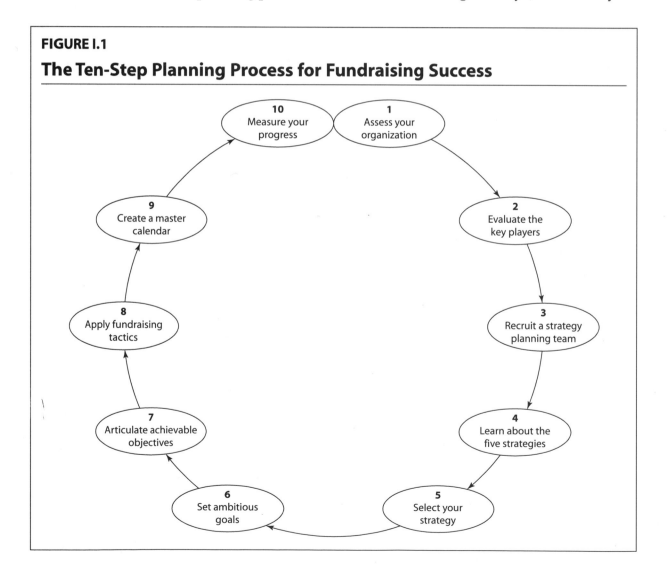

months), you'll be measuring your progress. But if you follow these ten steps, you will inevitably be led to a top-to-bottom review of your primary fundraising strategy. Every three years or so (or at critical junctures in your organization's history), you will begin the process over again, selecting a new strategy to reflect your organization's changed circumstances and new opportunities.

Along with this workbook, you'll find a CD-ROM that contains all of the exercises printed in this volume. This additional tool is especially useful for two reasons. First, you can complete the exercises on your computer screen and the scoring will happen automatically. Second, the computerized versions can be used to print out multiple copies of the exercises when they're being used to foster group discussion.

The ten steps to fundraising success won't solve all your fundraising problems, and they certainly won't compensate for any weaknesses that your organization has. But if you pursue the methodical course laid out in this workbook, we believe you stand a far better chance of identifying both your weaknesses and your strengths—and of making the most of both in a long-term effort to fulfill your organization's mission.

That, after all, is the reason we wrote this workbook. It's *your* mission, *your* goals, and *your* fundraising program. Only you can do what needs to be done. We hope we've made it just a little easier for you to do it.

Berkeley, California   Mal Warwick
September 2001   Stephen Hitchcock

Assess Your Organization's Current Fundraising Efforts

LET'S GET SOMETHING straight right off the bat: we assume your organization isn't perfect. We also believe you agree with that assumption, or you wouldn't be reading this workbook. If you're convinced your organization is a model for the nonprofit sector in every conceivable way, you've probably picked up the wrong book.

Truth to tell, nonprofit organizations are typically messy. Even the best of them tend to display numerous foibles and failings, and that's no wonder: most are underfunded, they depend heavily on volunteers, and more often than not they're run by youthful and inexperienced staff willing to work long hours at less than full wages.

Perfection is elusive at best in government and in the private sector too—but that's not our problem, at least not now. We're concerned here with the ways and means of strengthening nonprofit organizations.

That's why our *starting point* is to help you identify the problems your organization needs to address and solve. Step One will guide you through a hard-nosed assessment of your organization's strengths and weaknesses, so that you're fully aware of what's keeping some donors from supporting you as generously or as consistently as you (or they!) would like.

You may be able to boost your fundraising results by simply sweeping aside the obstacles that obstruct the generosity of your donors—and by displaying a more heartfelt and continuous sense of gratitude for their faithful (and often forgiving) support. But the long-term success of your organization and its fundraising programs will be more secure if you can tackle some of the fundamental flaws in your program and make strategic decisions that reflect both your organization's mission and your donors' interests.

Make every effort to tackle all of the exercises that follow. If you don't have enough information about a specific item, move on to the next question.

The purpose of this step is to give you an overall sense of your organization's readiness to engage in Steps Two through Ten.

Our point of departure in Step One is Exercise 1.1, "Ten Questions Every Nonprofit Board Member or Executive Needs to Answer." These ten questions help orient us to the fundraising environment of any nonprofit organization where we're about to become involved. Answering the same questions for your organization will help set you on the right path from the outset of your effort to evaluate your fundraising program.

In this exercise, enter 1 in the appropriate column if your answer is yes, 0 if your answer is no, and X if you're not sure. Then add up the number of Xs in the "Not Sure" column. If you checked "Not Sure" four or more times, you've got work to do. You're not ready to assess the health of your fundraising program. Do *not* add up your score! First, get the answers to those important questions.

If you answered at least seven of the ten basic questions, you can score your results. Multiply each score of 1 by the weight factor, and record the result in the column on the far right (the weight is 3 for each of the first eight basic questions and for question 10, and 1 for each of the three components of question 9). Add up the numbers in that column, and record the result in the box at the right-hand side of the last row. That's your score. Table 1.1 will help you interpret your score.

If any of these ten questions stumps you, we suggest you invest the effort to answer them before you go any further into this manual. You don't need to have satisfactory answers to every question at this early stage of the evaluation process. (In fact, it's a truly exceptional nonprofit organization that can answer all ten clearly and cheerfully!) What's important at this point is that you understand the significance of these strategic considerations. Your answers to the ten questions will set the stage for the more detailed evaluation this workbook will help you conduct.

Are You in the Right Business?

This is a workbook about fundraising, and that's why the first exercise focuses on that topic. But an organization's success—or failure—in raising money is actually a symptom of its overall health. Indeed, the continued existence of your organization is not guaranteed, nor is your claim to a share of public support either morally indisputable or derived from divine law.

No charity, cause, or institution can stay in business unless its leadership can forthrightly answer Yes! to each of the following seven questions:

1. Is your mission clearly defined?

2. Is it easy to demonstrate the current need for the work you do?

3. Is there a clearly defined constituency for your work?

EXERCISE 1.1

Ten Questions Every Nonprofit Board Member or Executive Needs to Answer

Question	Yes	No	Not Sure	Weight	Score
1. Are you raising more money every year?				× 3 =	
2. Does your funding come from several different sources, activities, or techniques, with no single source accounting for 60 percent or more? (Typical *sources* are foundations, corporations, special events, and the annual fund. Typical *techniques* are direct mail or planned giving.)				× 3 =	
3. Do you always have enough cash to pay your bills, plus a reserve fund to allow for contingencies?				× 3 =	
4. Does every member of your board without exception contribute money at least once a year?				× 3 =	
5. Is one senior-level person clearly designated as responsible for planning and monitoring your fundraising efforts?				× 3 =	
6. Are your financial resources scaled to match your organization's goals? In other words, can you honestly say your resources are adequate to match the scope of your ambitions, so that you're not greatly underfunded—or, conversely, that you don't command resources far in excess of what you require to accomplish your mission so that your organization is overfunded?				× 3 =	
7. Are you raising money from reliable, predictable sources, such as endowment income, membership dues, or monthly sustainer gifts, to cover your fixed expenses (that is, your overhead)? And if it's necessary, are you funding only variable expenses from less predictable sources, such as foundation grants, major gifts, or income from special appeals?				× 3 =	
8. Are your organization's fundraising activities scheduled in advance and carried out on time?				× 3 =	
9. Is your record-keeping system efficient and accurate?					
• Do you know how, where, and by whom your donor giving records are maintained, and what information is on file?				× 1 =	
• Do thank-you letters to your donors go out within seventy-two hours of the receipt of the gift and the same day for those who make major gifts?				× 1 =	
• Do you have the names and telephone numbers of your top ten or twenty donors at your fingertips?				× 1 =	
10. Does your organization have clearly understood policies on fundraising ethics, preferably in writing?				× 3 =	
Number answered "Not Sure"					
SCORE					_____

TABLE 1.1

Interpreting Your Score in Exercise 1.1

Number of Points	Interpretation
0–11	You're in trouble. Unless you make big changes, your organization will suffer—and probably sooner rather than later.
12–23	There are gaps in your development strategy. You need to take corrective action.
24–29	Not perfect, but you're in basically good shape. (It wouldn't hurt to address those weaknesses, anyway!)
30	Are you sure there isn't *something* you're doing wrong?

4. For your constituency, is yours the only organization that addresses your mission? In other words, do you fill a need that would otherwise go unfilled?

5. Are there people—either individually or through institutions such as foundations, corporations, or government agencies—willing to underwrite the cost of your work? In other words, is funding available, and do you know where and how to obtain it?

6. Are you serving people who would not otherwise be served, or pursuing a mission in the public interest that would not otherwise be fulfilled? In other words, are the taxpayers getting their money's worth?

7. Is there leadership in place to ensure that your organization will stick to its mission, serve its constituency, and honor ethical precepts and public interests?

This self-test helps establish whether your organization has legitimate claim to philanthropic support. In fact, your answers to these questions may lead you to conclude that the group you serve isn't ready for the process we describe in this workbook. You may have to attend to some basic issues of structure and mission before worrying about fundraising strategy.

Positioning Your Organization

Proper positioning is the first step to take before you solicit your next dollar, issue your next press release, or publish any other materials that describe your organization. Positioning is a way to make sure your mission meets real needs and will be valued by at least a meaningful portion of the public. You must be able to define what's unique about your organization and why anyone should support you.

A positioning statement will help you distinguish your organization from dozens or even thousands of others that do similar work. From the perspective of fundraising, the positioning statement is the case for giving in a nutshell. Exercise 1.2 will guide you through a simple process that will help you pin down the case.

Determining Your Message

Now that you've defined the essence of your case for giving through the positioning process laid out in Exercise 1.2, it's time to turn to the nitty-gritty details of the message you'll deliver in both written materials and conversations with your donors. That's the purpose of Exercise 1.3. Here are some questions to ask, consider, and then answer in preparing the material for your vision or case statement.

Enter a check to the right of each item once you've jotted down your answer to each of the forty-six questions in the exercise. Place a question mark there if you need more information to answer the question. If necessary, use the answer space to record notes about follow-up actions or assignments.

Your Record-Keeping Systems

Now is a good time to take stock of the record-keeping systems you have in place for your development program. An accurate, up-to-date record of all your fundraising transactions is just as important a fundraising tool as your case for giving.

Unless fewer than two hundred people are donors to your organization, you need a computer to keep track of all the necessary information about them and their gifts. Even if you have fewer than two hundred members or donors, there may be good reason to maintain a computer file. Fundraising is rife with details, and that means lots of bits and pieces of data.

Computers are much better at coping with data than we humans, no matter how good our memories might be. But computers offer more than mere memory power. And the computer, after all, is just one element in a record-keeping system. To help you get a handle on what you need in a back-end system, the list below indicates the ten features we think are most important:

1. Fast, accurate, and complete gift processing, with checks endorsed and deposited promptly to ensure that donor history is up-to-date and that no money is lost

2. Prompt gift acknowledgments—ideally, within twenty-four hours but within no more than seventy-two hours of receipt

3. Accurate, complete, and timely data entry to capture all the useful information about incoming contributions

EXERCISE 1.2

Positioning Your Organization: Does Your Mission Address Real Needs?

Section A	Check In with Your Mission

1. Write your current mission
    statement here.
    - Is this mission clear?
    - Does it still provide the right
      sense of direction for the future?

2. What changes, if any, should be
    considered in your mission?

Section B	Look at Needs and How You Will Address Them

For information to complete this section, turn first to your clients and staff. They're the best sources you have. However, sometimes staff and clients are too close to issues and existing programs to see what changes in focus could produce even greater impact. Add some outside perspective too.

1. List the most critical ongoing or
    emerging community needs you
    will address.

2. Outline ideas for how you might
    respond.

Section C	Survey the Competition to See How You Fit In

1. Who are your competitors?

2. What are you competing for?
    Donors and resources? Volunteers?
    Media attention?

3. How do your outstanding strengths
    compare with theirs?

4. List potential partners, and how
    you might team up with each.

There are four general ways competition affects decisions on positioning. After surveying the competition, how do things look for you? Check all those that apply:

- ❑ There are needs to be met, and we're exactly the people to do the job.
- ❑ It will be best to meet needs through a collaborative venture.
- ❑ Needs we identified are being met to some degree, but our contribution is necessary and unique, so we'll compete.
- ❑ The needs we identified are being met very well by others; we should back off.

Source: *This exercise is adapted from* Marketing Workbook for Nonprofit Organizations, Volume I: Develop the Plan, *by Gary J. Stern. Copyright © 1990 Amherst H. Wilder Foundation. Used with permission. For more information on Wilder Foundation publications call (800) 274–6024.*

EXERCISE 1.3

Forty-Six Questions to Ask in Preparing Your Case for Giving

How is your organization positioned in the community, and what is its heritage?

1. When was the organization founded?

2. What were the circumstances surrounding its beginnings?

3. What geographical area do you serve?

4. Are there natural resources in the area?

5. What is the industrial and business concentration in the area?

6. What distinguishes the area from the rest of the country, state, or nation (for example, is it a capital, a distribution center, a rural area)?

7. Describe the population of the service area.

8. What are the population trends (increasing or decreasing? aging?)?

9. What is the level of affluence, and what occupations stand out?

10. How would you characterize education levels in your area?

11. How does your organization benefit the community? How and whom does it serve?

12. What services do you offer?

13. How many people use these services? Have they recently increased or decreased? Why?

14. How much does each of these services cost? Are they furnished free or subsidized?

15. What are the services offered by other organizations in your area?

16. Is there any duplication of services, or is your organization's niche unique?

17. Do you cooperate with other organizations in joining programs or use of facilities?

18. In the community, is there a need for services not currently being met that the organization could fill if it had increased funds?

19. How many potential new users of the organization's services could you expect to attract if your programs were increased?

20. Why does the organization need funds?

21. Is the program for capital or endowment, or both?

22. What are the specific components of the campaign and project?

23. How will the campaign improve the organization's ability to fulfill its mission?

24. How much money do you need?

25. How will the money be raised?

26. What is the time frame for the campaign? Are there deadlines or significant anniversaries that should be taken into account?

27. Are there named gift opportunities and other means of donor recognition?

28. Have alternative sources of funding been investigated (such as government grants or bonds)?

Is the organization fiscally sound?

29. What is the current operating budget?

30. Is the institution in the black?

31. Who contributes the biggest share of the operating budget, and what percentage of the whole do those contributions constitute?

32. Does the organization have a membership drive, annual support campaign, admission fee, or subscriptions?

33. Do you have an endowment?

34. What are your financial assets and liabilities?

35. Are the investment management fees charged (if any) competitive?

36. Do you have a planned giving program?

Does the organization have strong leadership?

37. What is the composition of the board of directors (or trustees)?

38. How many people are on the board?

39. Are different ages and both sexes represented on the board?

40. Are major business and commercial interests represented on the board?

41. Are community minorities or the organization's constituency represented on the board?

42. Are staff members well qualified?

43. How many staff members are there?

44. What are the major strengths and accomplishments of the executive director and other key staff?

45. Does the organization use volunteers? Are they effective?

46. Do the administrative facilities meet the requirements of the staff and volunteers?

Source: *Copyright © 1995 by Jerold Panas, Linzy & Partners, Inc. Adapted with permission.*

4. Segmentation options so you can select and group donors into smaller subsets according to their patterns of giving or other common characteristics

5. Multidimensional reports on your donor file that are produced on a regular schedule (weekly or monthly), giving you perspective on the performance of your fundraising program on at least a monthly basis

6. Variable output options, so you can produce data in standardized formats to use in gift receipts, statistical reports, mailing labels, and personalized letters either from your own system or on diskettes or e-mail transmissions so that vendors can produce your mailings

7. Extra information about major gift prospects, to allow fundraising staff to store and retrieve the personal data they need for face-to-face solicitations

8. Fast access to gift histories, so you can field inquiries from donors, rank donors for major gift campaigns, prepare staff or volunteers for direct solicitations, or help organize special events

9. Security, to protect against loss from theft or fire and to guard against unauthorized use of your list

10. Archival record keeping, allowing you to maintain permanent records of out-of-date information while keeping your active donor list lean and useful

Most nonprofit organizations find all ten of these characteristics essential. Even if your back-end system already offers all these features, don't consider yourself perfect. Instead, think of this list as a starting point.

The Ethics Self-Test

Nonprofit enterprises are doubly blessed with public support: they receive tax exemption, and they are given the designation as worthy charities or public interest organizations. In turn, those groups are morally obligated to hold to the highest standards of ethical conduct. The ethics self-test in Exercise 1.4 will help you explore the ethical dimensions of your governance and resource development programs.

You can use this exercise to identify any problems or outstanding questions that need attention. If you enter follow-up or corrective steps to take in the spaces labeled "Action," this self-test can help move ethics even higher up on the priority list of your fundraising program.

To complete this exercise, enter a check mark in the appropriate column ("Yes," "No," or "Not Sure"). Then note the necessary follow-up or corrective actions in the spaces marked "Action."

EXERCISE 1.4

Does Your Organization Pass the Ethics Self-Test?

Question	Yes	No	Not Sure
1. Is there a governing board of trustees or directors on which nonemployees outnumber employees by at least two to one? (A nonprofit organization that is a subsidiary or a dependency of another nonprofit may do just fine without its own independent board. In such cases, apply this question to the parent organization.) ACTION:			
2. Do you have a written policy on fundraising ethics and conflict of interest? ACTION:			
3. Are all directors or trustees free of financial self-interest? ACTION:			
4. Do all the written materials you distribute to potential donors or the public at large accurately and honestly present your mission, track record, and current priorities? ACTION:			
5. Do your financial statements fairly and accurately represent the realities of your current financial situation? ACTION:			
6. Does your organization "own" your list of donors? In other words, is your staff free to determine when and how communications may be directed to your donors or members, and who will be authorized to do so? ACTION:			
7. Are there written contracts for all fundraising work performed by agencies or individuals who are not employed on your staff? ACTION:			

(Continued)

EXERCISE 1.4   *(Continued)*

Question	Yes	No	Not Sure
8. Are all fundraising personnel, agencies, or consultants compensated exclusively on the basis of work performed for your organization? (This rules out fees pegged to results obtained and rights to the use of your donor list—but not necessarily a system of bonuses for exceptional performance.) ACTION:			
9. Is your resource development program based on a thoughtful, balanced strategy that you can honestly say will enable you to secure financial support over the long term in the most cost-effective manner possible? ACTION:			
10. Is your governing board free to use all funds raised to support your organization's mission? (This rules out accepting gifts earmarked for purposes not clearly within the bounds of your mission but does not necessarily exclude raising money for designated purposes that are consistent with the mission.) ACTION:			

There really is not a score for this exercise because there is no such thing as conduct that's "sort of ethical." If you answered no or not sure to any of these ten questions, you've got work to do!

Conclusion

Now that you've completed Step One, identifying your organization's biggest strengths and weaknesses, it's time to turn to Step Two, where we will continue the assessment process. The exercises and suggestions in Step Two will help you evaluate your board members, executive director, development director—in other words, those who will play a role in carrying out your organization's fundraising strategy.

Assess the Fundraising Strengths and Weaknesses of Your Board Members and Staff

WE'RE NOT GOING to tell which author is which, but the two of us have had an ongoing disagreement that has lasted for nearly two decades. One of us has at least ten good ideas before he's finished breakfast. The other of us typically responds, "That's a great idea, and you've even thought about how to get it done. But I'm less interested in what to do and how to do it than in *who* is going to do it and why that person will want to do it."

Of course, we're both right when it comes to fundraising success. You must have great ideas—the right strategy, if you will—as well as some sense about the objectives and tactics to fulfill that strategy. But if you're to choose the best strategy for your organization, you must know the strengths and weaknesses of those who will do this work. The exercises in Step One gave you a sense of your organization's health. Now, in Step Two, you'll assess the capabilities of those who must shape your strategy (especially those who might serve on your strategy team, outlined in Step Three) as well as those who will be essential to implementing the strategy you select.

There are at least two interrelated reasons to make this assessment at this stage, before you actually select your strategy:

1. Choosing the right fundraising strategy means that your team has picked a course of action that builds on the strengths and interests of those who are most likely to carry it out.

2. When your strategy team makes its recommendation to the governing board and senior leadership, you will want to include specific

suggestions about changes and additions that need to be made in staffing and volunteers in order to implement the strategy.

To be sure, evaluating board members and staff will create some tension and conflict. But selecting a strategy is ultimately about changing your organization—moving it from one place to a more effective place. You wouldn't be serving on the fundraising strategy team unless you believe that your organization needs to discover a new course of action and that it must have the courage to make the necessary changes to pursue that new strategy. The exercises in this step will help you examine the effectiveness of the key players in this important undertaking.

How Well Is Your Board Doing Its Job?

The National Center for Nonprofit Boards estimates that nearly two and a half million Americans sit on the governing bodies of nonprofit causes and institutions. It has calculated the average board size as nineteen members.

How many of those people govern—and how many just sit? Exercise 2.1 will help you get a handle on how well the directors of your organization are performing their duties.

It's a good idea to assess board and key staff members every year. Some organizations find it useful for a form like this one to be distributed to each board member for a self-assessment. In addition, the board chair, the executive committee, or the special board development committee may also conduct an independent assessment of how well the board is doing its job.

To complete the exercise, assign a score to your board from 1 to 10 (1 = poor, 5 = acceptable, 10 = outstanding) for each of the factors listed, and write it in the column labeled "Score." Then score the results:

1. Multiply the score for each question by the weight factor in the column next to it. The weightiest factors are listed first. Write the result in the far-right column. That will be a number from 1 to 50.

2. Add up the scores in the far-right column. If you assigned your organization a top (or "perfect") score of 10 for every factor, the result will be 430.

Table 2.1 shows how to interpret your score.

Evaluating Your Executive Director

There isn't a nonprofit organization on the face of this planet that will flourish unless its chief executive officer supports the fundraising effort. To set the stage for selecting the best fundraising strategy, you'll need to take a

EXERCISE 2.1

How Well Is Your Board Doing Its Job?

Factor	Score	Weight	Total
1. Does the board include a majority of observant and vocal independent members (without financial ties to the institution) to ensure that the public interest is protected?		× 3 =	
2. Does the board, one of its committees, or its chairperson supervise and consult with the chief executive officer on a regular basis?		× 3 =	
3. Does every member of the board make what is for that person a generous cash gift at least once a year?		× 3 =	
4. Is there a board development process in place through which board members' performance is evaluated, new board prospects are identified and recruited, and the character of the board as a whole evolves, as necessary, to meet the organization's changing needs?		× 3 =	
5. Are terms of office for the board written into the by-laws and enforced by the leadership, so the board renews its membership on a regular cycle?		× 3 =	
6. Do board members act strictly in the organization's best interest, setting aside their own personal interests (or those of other institutions they may be connected with)?		×3 =	
7. Does the board provide on an annual basis a formal review of the performance of the chief executive officer, and without meddling or micromanaging?		× 3 =	
8. Does the board possess skills or provide access to contacts and resources that staff members do not possess or have access to?		× 2 =	
9. Do board members keep their commitments, completing tasks they're assigned or fulfilling the promises they make?		× 2 =	
10. Does the board provide leadership in fundraising activities by actively participating in events, writing letters of support to foundations or corporations, or in other tangible ways?		× 2 =	
11. Does the board meet at least four times annually? If not, does an elected executive committee of the board meet at least four times annually?		× 2 =	
12. Do members regularly attend meetings of the board (and, if appropriate, board committees)?		× 2 =	
13. Is the board actively and regularly involved in reviewing the budget and financial performance of the organization?		× 2 =	
14. Are members of the board vigilant about maintaining high ethical standards for the organization? If the circumstances		× 2 =	

(Continued)

EXERCISE 2.1 *(Continued)*

Factor	Score	Weight	Total
demand, do they ask questions or make comments, in either board meetings or conversations with the chief executive or other senior staff members?			
15. Does the board (or one of its committees) play an active, ongoing role in strategic planning?		× 2 =	
16. Are all major stakeholder groups (such as the organization's clients, patrons, members or donors, staff, and the public) effectively represented on the board?		× 1 =	
17. Is the board (or, if necessary, an executive committee) small enough to conduct frank and productive meetings?		× 1 =	
18. Do board members prepare for meetings and participate in discussions?		× 1 =	
19. Do board members understand and value the organization's mission? Do they understand the connection between mission and programs?		× 1 =	
20. Are members of the board accessible to the chief executive officer (and, if appropriate, other staff members) for advice and assistance?		× 1 =	
21. Does the board as a whole reflect the ethnic, racial, and economic diversity of your community and your constituency?		× 1 =	
SCORE			_____

TABLE 2.1

Interpreting Your Score in Exercise 2.1

Score	Interpretation
38–100	This organization has major problems! Addressing other pressing matters (such as fundraising or lack of strategic planning) must take a back seat to board development. Just hope it isn't too late!
101–200	Board development must be a high priority for this organization. There's a lot of work to do!
201–300	This organization is basically healthy—but there's room for improvement in the board. Review the weak spots carefully. Address them as opportunities arise.
301–429	If there were an organizational equivalent of Mensa, the group for people with high IQs, this institution would qualify for automatic admission! (But that's no reason to slack off! Why not go for perfection?)
430	Clearly, this organization is one in a million—and you're probably an extra-generous person as well!

close look at the fundraising role and attitudes of your executive director, president, executive vice president (or whatever you call the person on whose desk, after all, the buck stops).

Exercise 2.2 addresses this issue. Make a copy of this exercise for the executive director. You may wish to use it in a parallel self-evaluation.

Assign a score from 1 to 10 (1 = poor, 5 = acceptable, 10 = outstanding) to your chief executive for each of the criteria indicated in the column labeled "Factor" and write it in the column labeled "Score." To score the exercise:

1. Multiply the score you've assigned for each question by the weight factor, if any, in the column next to it. The weightiest factors are listed first. Write the result in the far-right column. That will be a number from 1 to 30.

2. Add up the resulting scores in the far-right column. If you assigned your chief executive a top (or "perfect") score of 10 for every factor, the result will be 210.

Use Table 2.2 to interpret your score.

Evaluating Your Development Director

A plan means little unless someone puts it into practice. In fact, some of the best-crafted fundraising plans we've seen have produced nothing for the charities that adopted them. In one case, the problem lay in the top-down process that produced the plan. The people responsible for doing the work had been excluded. In another case, the development director was simply not up to the job. There's no getting around it: you can't separate fundraising from fundraisers.

Exercise 2.3 will help you assess the fitness of the person in charge of your fundraising program. If there isn't such a person—either a paid staff person or a designated volunteer in charge of fundraising—there ought to be. This may not always be a full-time position, but the person must be fully responsible for resource development.

In Exercise 2.3, assign a score to your development director from 1 to 10 (1 = poor, 5 = acceptable, 10 = outstanding) for each of the criteria listed in the column labeled "Factor," and write it in the column labeled "Score." To score the exercise:

1. Multiply the score assigned for each question by the weight factor in the column next to it. The weightiest factors are listed first. Write the result in the far-right column. That will be a number from 1 to 50.

EXERCISE 2.2

Evaluating Your Executive Director

	Factor	Score	Weight	Total
1.	Is vigilant (and, if necessary, outspoken) about maintaining high ethical standards for the organization		× 5 =	
2.	Is accountable to the board, meeting or exceeding measurable goals as assessed in an annual review conducted by the board chair (and personnel committee, if any)		× 3 =	
3.	Knows enough about fundraising methods to help the development staff decide whether and how those methods might be useful for the organization		× 3 =	
4.	Views fundraising from a strategic perspective, with the fundraising program serving a larger organizational purpose and with individual techniques and funding sources (major gifts, direct mail, planned giving) performing complementary functions		× 2 =	
5.	Addresses problems and makes decisions on matters related to fundraising after careful consultation with key affected staff members in an open, honest, and professional way		× 2 =	
6.	Is able, when called on, to motivate board, staff, volunteers, and donors to contribute meaningfully to the fundraising program		× 1 =	
7.	Is accessible to the director of development (and, if appropriate, other staff members) for advice and assistance		× 1 =	
8.	Participates actively in fundraising, or provides access to donors and resources that aren't accessible to the development staff on its own		× 1 =	
9.	Is deeply committed to the organization's mission and continually reminds board, staff, and volunteers to remain focused on the mission		× 1 =	
10.	Makes a significant personal cash gift to the organization at least once a year		× 1 =	
11.	Ensures that adequate resources (such as e-mail, meetings, bulletins, and newsletters) are devoted to keeping lines of communication open among staff members		× 1 =	
	SCORE			

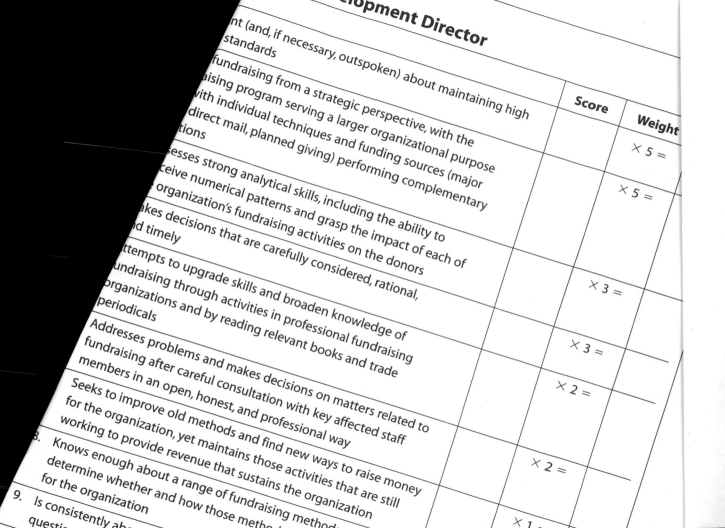

...lopment Director

...nt (and, if necessary, outspoken) about maintaining high standards

...fundraising from a strategic perspective, with the ...ising program serving a larger organizational purpose

...with individual techniques and funding sources (major direct mail, planned giving) performing complementary ...tions

...esses strong analytical skills, including the ability to ...ceive numerical patterns and grasp the impact of each of ...organization's fundraising activities on the donors ...kes decisions that are carefully considered, rational, ...d timely

...ttempts to upgrade skills and broaden knowledge of ...undraising through activities in professional fundraising ...organizations and by reading relevant books and trade periodicals

Addresses problems and makes decisions on matters related to fundraising after careful consultation with key affected staff members in an open, honest, and professional way

Seeks to improve old methods and find new ways to raise money for the organization, yet maintains those activities that are still working to provide revenue that sustains the organization

8. Knows enough about a range of fundraising method... determine whether and how those metho... for the organization

9. Is consistently ab... questi...

	Score	Weight
		× 5 =
		× 5 =
		× 3 =
		× 3 =
		× 2 =
		× 2 =
		× 1 =

The information provided in Table 2.2 is incorrect. Please use the following guidelines when interpreting your score in Exercise 2.2.

TABLE 2.2

Interpreting Your Score in Exercise 2.2

Score	Interpretation
21–30	You can't fix your fundraising problems without replacing this person.
31–60	There are problems here. The board will have to assess whether these are shortcomings that can be remedied or worked around in some way.
61–80	Falls short in several key areas. An intense performance review is called for with an agreement for systematic training and reevaluation in the future.
81–104	You're getting your money's worth, and more! This executive lends strength to the fundraising program.
105	Are you *sure*? If so, don't fail to let her know what a great job she's doing!

TABLE 2.2

Interpreting Your Score in Exercise 2.2

Score	Interpretation
27–70	It's time for this person to go. Otherwise your fun...
71–110	Take a close look at this person's performance. De... organization and the individual would be better of...
111–160	This person doesn't quite measure up. Try a perform... suggest the person attend training programs to impr...
161–209	It's extremely difficult to find the truly well-rounded d... isn't quite perfect isn't cause for alarm. Her strengths in... you pay for her weaknesses in other areas.
210	A real gem!

2. Add up the resulting scores in the far... your organization a top (or "perfect") s... result will be 280.

To interpret your development director's s...

Using a Consultant to Strengthen Your ...ing Efforts

...ganization may already be using one or m... ...f your development program. Or... ...u may have concluded... ...available in y...

TABLE 2.2

Interpreting Your Score in Exercise 2.2

Score	Interpretation
27–70	It's time for this person to go. Otherwise your fundraising program will continue to suffer.
71–110	Take a close look at this person's performance. Decide whether, all things considered, the organization and the individual would be better off with someone else in this job.
111–160	This person doesn't quite measure up. Try a performance review or a heart-to-heart talk, and suggest the person attend training programs to improve knowledge and skills.
161–209	It's extremely difficult to find the truly well-rounded development director. Just because yours isn't quite perfect isn't cause for alarm. Her strengths in one area may be well worth the price you pay for her weaknesses in other areas.
210	A real gem!

2. Add up the resulting scores in the far-right column. If you assigned your organization a top (or "perfect") score of 10 for every factor, the result will be 280.

To interpret your development director's score, consult Table 2.3.

Using a Consultant to Strengthen Your Fundraising Efforts

Your organization may already be using one or more consultants to assist with part or all of your development program. Or as a result of reviewing Steps One and Two, you may have concluded that you need some more wisdom and experience than is available in your current board or staff. In either case, the skills and experience of any consultants, and how well your organization makes use of those, should be part of your assessment of your organization's strengths and weaknesses. Exercise 2.4 will help you evaluate any current consultants or any prospects you might be interested in engaging to help you with this planning process or to implement your plans once you've completed these ten steps. With this evaluation in hand, you'll be better equipped to pick the strategy that's right for your organization.

In Exercise 2.4, we've left space below each tip for you to enter notes as appropriate. Each point will force you to make a judgment call. There are few hard-and-fast rules that apply to hiring a fundraising consultant—except one: be sure the consultant is honest and sensitive to the ethical dimensions of the job and the relationship with you.

EXERCISE 2.3

Evaluating Your Development Director

	Factor	Score	Weight	Total
1.	Is vigilant (and, if necessary, outspoken) about maintaining high ethical standards		× 5 =	
2.	Views fundraising from a strategic perspective, with the fundraising program serving a larger organizational purpose and with individual techniques and funding sources (major gifts, direct mail, planned giving) performing complementary functions		× 5 =	
3.	Possesses strong analytical skills, including the ability to perceive numerical patterns and grasp the impact of each of the organization's fundraising activities on the donors		× 3 =	
4.	Makes decisions that are carefully considered, rational, and timely		× 3 =	
5.	Attempts to upgrade skills and broaden knowledge of fundraising through activities in professional fundraising organizations and by reading relevant books and trade periodicals		× 2 =	
6.	Addresses problems and makes decisions on matters related to fundraising after careful consultation with key affected staff members in an open, honest, and professional way		× 2 =	
7.	Seeks to improve old methods and find new ways to raise money for the organization, yet maintains those activities that are still working to provide revenue that sustains the organization		× 1 =	
8.	Knows enough about a range of fundraising methods to determine whether and how those methods might be useful for the organization		× 1 =	
9.	Is consistently above reproach in any matters in which ethical questions might arise		× 1 =	
10.	Listens well and commands any necessary supervisory skills		× 1 =	
11.	Is able, when called on, to motivate board, staff, volunteers, and donors to contribute meaningfully to the fundraising program		× 1 =	
12.	Ensures that adequate resources (such as e-mail, meetings, bulletins, and newsletters) are devoted to keeping lines of communication open among development staff members		× 1 =	
13.	Is accessible to donors, board members, and subordinate staff		× 1 =	
14.	Makes a personal cash gift to the organization at least once annually		× 1 =	
	SCORE			_____

TABLE 2.3

Interpreting Your Score in Exercise 2.3

Score	Interpretation
27–90	It's time for this person to go. Otherwise, your fundraising program will continue to suffer.
91–160	Take a close look at this person's performance. Decide whether, all things considered, the organization and the individual would be better off with someone else in this job.
161–240	This person doesn't quite measure up. Try a performance review or a heart-to-heart talk, and suggest the person attend training programs to improve knowledge and skills.
241–279	It's extremely difficult to find the truly well-rounded development director. Just because yours isn't quite perfect isn't cause for alarm. His strengths in one area may be well worth the price you pay for his weaknesses in other areas.
280	A real gem!

EXERCISE 2.4

Ten Tips for Hiring a Consultant

	Tip
1.	Carefully identify the problem to be addressed. Identifying symptoms may mislead the consultant.
2.	Make sure you have a clear picture of the desired result of the consultant's work.
3.	Be sure your organization, particularly top management, is committed to change.
4.	Ask friends, colleagues, and staff in other nonprofits in your community and associations for recommendations.
5.	Develop a standard format for proposals.
6.	Check the consultant's references.
7.	Make sure the consultant's procedures and techniques are suited to your organization.

(Continued)

EXERCISE 2.4 *(Continued)*

Tip

---

8. If you are hiring a consulting firm, know exactly who will be doing the work with your organization.

9. Check the data the consultant uncovers.

10. Always put the agreement between your organization and the consultant in writing.

Source: *Adapted with permission from* CAN Alert, *the newsletter of the California Association of Nonprofits (May 1, 1995 Volume 9/ Number 3) Copyright ©1995 California Association of Nonprofits.*

Conclusion

Now that you've taken a reading of your organization's health and have evaluated those who will play a key role in implementing your fundraising, it's time to use Step Three to recruit a team of people who will take the lead in a process designed to select the best fundraising strategy for your organization.

Assemble the Team to Select the Best Fundraising Strategy

NOW THAT YOU'VE had a chance to assess the state of your organization and evaluate some of its key players, you're probably eager to read on—to find out how to fix those problems and set things on their proper course. We'd be pleased (and flattered!) if you kept reading and filling out all the forms and checklists on the pages ahead. But our real hope is that you'll stop using this workbook on your own. Rather than keep reading by yourself, we encourage you to assemble a working group, task force, or team of people to be responsible for selecting your organization's fundraising strategy. As we've worked with dozens and dozens of organizations for over two decades, we have become convinced that almost every nonprofit is more likely to pick the right strategy for fundraising when it makes that selection as the result of a deliberate discussion that involves key stakeholders in the organization. This strategy planning team would agree to follow a process that we believe will help you choose the single best fundraising strategy for your organization at this stage in its development.

Some Preliminary Considerations

We suggest you plan on anywhere from three to six separate sessions devoted to choosing a fundraising strategy. Ideally, each of those sessions will last two to three hours, probably with a break in the middle. Our experience is that sessions that go on for more than three hours produce diminishing returns. Remember that this is about *choosing* the best strategy—not discussing it to death.

An alternative is a two-day retreat. During the two days, there would be three to six sessions, each lasting two to three hours each. Participants could use the free time between sessions for reading the workbook and for personal reflection.

If you're using this workbook for a periodic evaluation of your strategy, two or three sessions might be enough.

Choosing Team Members

Whether you're doing this for the first time or taking stock of your current fundraising plan, Exercise 3.1 will help you select the people who could best serve on your fundraising strategy team. Use this exercise to review potential participants on your strategy planning team according to the four criteria we believe are most critical for success:

- The individual's number of years with the organization
- The individual's availability for meetings
- The individual's knowledge of the mission
- The individual's willingness to listen.

We have suggested eleven possible participants (or classes of participants), which are listed in the first column.

To complete Exercise 3.1, write in the names of those individuals you want to consider actively. In the next column, note the number of years the individual has been associated with your agency. Then place a check mark in the columns to the right of each name to indicate whether that person fulfills each of the key criteria in turn.

When assessing the results of this exercise, you may be well advised to seek balance between old-timers and neophytes. You'll also want to benefit from experience as well as gain a fresh perspective by recruiting both those who understand the organization's mission and those who don't.

We aren't afraid to include someone with less than comprehensive knowledge of fundraising or an organization's history. The strategy team needs participants who can ask "stupid questions" and offer wild ideas. If everyone keeps saying, "We tried that before and it didn't work," then you're *unlikely* to pick a strategy that will drive your fundraising into the future. Ultimately, the board of directors must adopt this strategy, and the staff must implement it, so there are plenty of safeguards.

In assembling your balanced yet bold strategy team, don't make the mistake of including anyone who is unavailable for meetings or unwilling to listen to others. Your group should include:

- At least five individuals willing to attend all sessions to make sure there's enough discussion from a variety of viewpoints

EXERCISE 3.1

Assessing the Prospects for Your Fundraising Strategy Team

	Name	Number of Years with Organization	Available for Meetings	Knows Mission	Willing to Listen
Chief executive					
Board chair					
Development committee chair					
Client or participant in one of the organization's programs					
Graduate or past participant in the organization					
A leader from another group in the community					
A professor, researcher, or planning official knowledgeable about your community or issue					
Director of development					
Person responsible for gift processing					
Long-time donor					
New donor					
Other					

- No more than twelve participants so that team members can be comfortable with each other and make decisions
- At least two individuals other than top senior staff
- At least two senior decision-making staff members
- At least one member of the board of directors

As you review the prospects to serve, be sure that no one individual will be likely to dominate the discussion. If the executive director or the board chair is a meeting hog, it's better to meet with that person one-on-one and keep him or her informed of the strategy team's progress.

Selecting the Chairperson of Your Strategy Team

Once you've recruited those you want to include on the strategy team, you're ready to select the right chairperson for your team. We believe the director of development is *not* the best person to convene and chair the fundraising strategy team. It's all too easy to get defensive about the organization's current fundraising endeavors, and the development staff has a full-time role in supporting both the chair of the strategy team and other team members.

The ideal chairperson for your fundraising strategy team should have the following qualities:

- An understanding of and commitment to your organization's mission

- An awareness of or active involvement in the community, issue, or arena addressed by your organization

- A willingness to listen to others, especially those with different opinions

- The ability to summarize wide-ranging information quickly and simply

- A strong desire to get the job done, including setting time limits on discussion so that your team can actually select a strategy

Establishing the Process for Choosing Your Fundraising Strategy

Now you're ready to turn your attention to the nuts and bolts of the team meeting process. To make sure that discussions are as productive as possible, turn Table 3.1, which provides a checklist of arrangements and guidelines for the environment in which your work is conducted.

Taking too little or too much time are both pitfalls. You want to make sure adequate consideration has been given to your organization's options, and that takes time. Include time between meetings so that each participant can mull over the discussion and decisions of the previous session—but not so much time that participants feel that they're starting from scratch at the next meeting.

Your goal is to choose a strategy and then get to work on implementing it. Aiming for perfection is very dangerous. If you take too long to select your strategy, you won't have time to implement it—and then learn in the

TABLE 3.1

Fostering the Right Environment to Encourage Discussion

Item

1. A comfortable, quiet meeting room that is easily accessible to team members. Nonprofit organizations often lack pleasant and productive meeting rooms. Alternatives include:

   - A conference room in the local library or community center.
   - Meeting rooms at a city club, university club, or athletic club.
   - A private dining room in a restaurant.
   - A conference room of a team member's business.
   - A meeting room in a church or synagogue. (Be careful that you don't end up in the dreary basement.)

2. Conduct your meetings in a friendly but businesslike fashion:

   - Start on time and finish on time (or even ten minutes early).
   - Provide breakfast, lunch, or dinner for at least the first session (to express appreciation for the team's participation and encourage members to get to know one another).
   - Set up a round table (if there are as few as five team members) or tables in a horseshoe shape so that everyone can face each other.
   - Have copies of this workbook or relevant worksheets from the CD-ROM for each team member.
   - Secure one or more flip charts with pads of writing paper so that group notes can be recorded.

3. At the first meeting, set some simple ground rules—for example:

   - Express opinions and provide honest answers.
   - Respect confidentiality of information about finances, donors, and clients.
   - Keep comments as concise as possible so others have an opportunity to talk.
   - Don't rush to judgment. Wait until the group has gone through the process before latching on to one strategy.
   - Don't seek perfection or a timeless strategy. Trust that an informal, wide-ranging discussion will result in the best strategy given the current circumstances.
   - For every hour of discussion, make sure the group uses at least one of the exercises (to focus the discussion and to give opportunities for each individual to contribute his or her assessment).
   - At the beginning and end of each session, take five minutes to summarize where you are in the process.

implementation state what you need to change to become even more effective. So we recommend no more than three months for the entire process.

You'll find below a step-by-step outline that could serve as a model for you to adopt to your strategy team's planning sessions. Our outline assumes you'll have three separate sessions of three hours each. The first session might include a meal and an opportunity for team members to get to know each other. You may wish to tackle this work in a series of five or six shorter meetings of ninety minutes or two hours. (One-hour sessions don't allow enough time for give-and-take.) And even if you're able to schedule three-hour sessions, you may decide to break up the third session into two separate meetings. Some organizations (especially those without professional staff who are responsible for implementation) may need to spend more time identifying the specific goals, achievable objectives, and appropriate tactics.

As you and your strategy team follow the outline below, take time for discussion, and allow each individual to offer comments or raise questions. But at the same time, encourage team members to keep moving through the process. The task at hand is *not* to resolve all of your organization's problems or to pick the perfect strategy. Rather, the purpose here is to select—within a realistic time frame—the best possible fundraising strategy for your organization at this point in its history.

Session One

1. Distribute copies of the workbook to each participant.

2. Have the team members introduce themselves, describe their connection to the organization, and tell "one thing about themselves that's not obvious" (or another ice-breaker activity).

3. Take time for individuals to complete at least three of the exercises from Steps One and Two. Using a flip chart or other means, record what the planning team believes are the organization's five chief strengths and its five greatest weaknesses.

4. As a group, review "Overview of the Five Strategies," in Step Four.

5. For each of the five strategies outlined in "Why Pursuing *One* Strategy Is Essential" (Step Four, pp. 39–42), discuss a specific application to your organization.

6. Possible homework: Encourage team members to read the workbook Introduction, complete all of the exercises in Steps One and Two, and review once again the "Overview of the Five Strategies" in Step Four.

Session Two

7. Restate the highlights of Session One.

8. Take time for comments and questions from those who have read the first four chapters of this workbook.

9. Complete Exercise 5.1: "Which Fundraising Strategy Is Right for Your Organization?"

10. Ask each participant in the group to explain which of the Five Strategies is *not* an appropriate one for your organization.

11. Record on the flip chart the one strategy chosen by each participant.

12. Seek some consensus or broad agreement on the one strategy that's right for your organization at this time. See the suggestions on pages 45–46 if you're having trouble achieving consensus on the right primary strategy for your organization.

13. Summarize.

14. Possible homework: Ask team members to pretend that the strategy they've chosen is now unavailable. Have each individual select his or her *next-best* strategy—and jot down notes about why that one was a second favorite. Encourage team members to read Steps Five and Six.

Session Three

15. Restate the conclusions reached at the previous session.

16. Ask participants to report on their choices of the next-best strategy in the event that the first one isn't available. Double-check to make sure that there's still consensus on the primary strategy chosen in the previous session.

17. Complete Exercise 5.2: "Choosing Your Secondary Fundraising Strategy."

18. Use the exercises in Step Six to set ambitious new goals that reflect your organization's newly chosen strategy. (You may need to schedule an additional session or sessions if your organization is new, large, or multifaceted.)

19. Go back and ask the group to identify any goals that are *not* essential to achieving your overarching fundraising strategy.

20. Record on the flip chart your organization's strategy and your major goals for the next three to five years.

21. Select two or three team members who will meet with the development staff to review the objectives they set and the tactics they propose to achieve those objectives (Steps Six and Seven). Your organization's professional staff may also wish to consult with the smaller team as they schedule fundraising activities (Step Nine).

22. Agree to meet in six months to review the organization's progress in implementing the primary and secondary fundraising strategies (Step Ten).

23. Thank the participants!

24. Possible homework: Read Steps Seven through Ten, and write down observations that could be useful to the organization's professional

staff—to assist them as they develop objectives, fundraising programs, and schedules to implement the goals set by the strategy team.

Action Steps

After reviewing all the recommendations in this step, you'll need to take some specific actions:

1. Contact those you've decided are the best candidates to serve on the fundraising strategy planning team. Secure their agreement to be on the team, and provide a brief explanation of their role and responsibilities.

2. Arrange a comfortable place, and set dates and times for your team to meet.

3. Secure copies of your organization's mission statement, the most recent annual report, and a brief description of your current fundraising activities, as well as copies of this workbook for each team member.

4. Send out written invitations to the team members, including a map or directions to the meeting location.

Conclusion

Once you've taken these steps, you're really ready for the fun part: selecting the one strategy that will help your organization achieve success in fundraising. First, though, you and your strategy team members will want to review Step Four. You'll learn about the five fundamental strategies for organizations like yours. You'll also get a chance to weigh the costs and benefits of each of those five strategies.

Weigh the Costs and Benefits of the Five Strategies for Fundraising Success

AT THIS POINT, you have put together a strategy planning team. You may even have had your initial meeting and have taken some measure of your organization's fundraising efforts. You and your members may have reached one of three conclusions:

1. You're troubled that things aren't quite on track. There are real challenges you need to face, and you'd better deal with them soon.

2. Your current situation is rosy, but it seems likely that your organization will face some big problems ahead. You know your good fortune can't last forever, because circumstances beyond your organization's control can dramatically affect your future income.

3. You're lucky enough to work for an organization that doesn't have to worry about fundraising.

If the third choice describes your situation, you may close this workbook, place it on a shelf, and smile smugly every time you notice it as you go on with your work. But if either of the first two conclusions is closer to the mark, you'd be wise to continue making your way through the remaining steps.

Whatever your situation—high anxiety, mild concern, or thoughtful consideration of the future—you'll benefit from a disciplined determination of your organization's fundraising strategy. That's how Step Four can help you and the strategy planning team you assembled in Step Three. By following the step-by-step process in this chapter, you'll understand more fully exactly what fundraising strategies are available to your organization. You'll also gain a sense of the costs and benefits and the advantages and disadvantages of the principal strategies any group can pursue.

The authors have worked with hundreds of groups over nearly three decades, and we've come to see that there are fundamentally five strategies that are truly effective in achieving success in fundraising: Growth, Involvement, Visibility, Efficiency, and Stability (abbreviated GIVES).

Overview of the Five Strategies

The easy way to remember the five strategies is in the sequence: Growth, Involvement, Visibility, Efficiency, Stability. That way, their initial letters spell out a nifty little mnemonic device: GIVES.

To lend more meaning to that simple exercise, we've summed up the characteristics of the five strategies in the table that follows. Note that the attributes and examples cited are only to illustrate the broad-brush characteristics of the five strategies, and just because we use one organization as a "typical example," don't assume that this is the ideal strategy for that type of organization. For instance, there are lots of universities that shouldn't pursue a strategy of stability. Each organization is unique, and every organization's fundraising needs change over time.

Strategy	G Growth	I Involvement	V Visibility	E Efficiency	S Stability
Core attribute	Dynamic	Rewarding	Familiar	Resourceful	Enduring
Characteristics	Audacious goals, bold leadership, low entry-level gift	Volunteer programs, grassroots lobbying	Broad public interest, public opinion is key, many stakeholders, brand identification	Cost-conscious, well-established	Unchanging values, unending needs, broad financial base
Representative tactics	Direct mail acquisition	Direct mail membership, telephone fundraising, donor newsletters, welcome packages	TV/radio, special events, cause-related marketing, publications	Planned giving, major gifts, foundations, corporations, monthly giving, workplace giving, government grants	Endowment, diversified fundraising, electronic fund transfer
Typical examples	Environmental groups, animal rights organizations, anything new	Museums, performing arts organizations, public policy groups	Medical research organizations, emergency relief charities	Social service agencies, hospitals	Universities and colleges, residential care facilities
Mission requires . . .	Broad reach, substantial impact	Public participation	Broad public awareness and understanding, name recognition, action	Frugal management	Sound finances, cash reserves, long-term perspective

What Is Strategy?

Strategy is where you want your organization to be in the future. Given your commitment to your organization's mission and your assessment of your strengths and weaknesses, what do you hope will be true about your agency at some distant, but not remote, point?

Strategy is *not* about how you get from here to there, but rather a description of where "there" is. If what you come up with looks a lot like your current situation, then you don't have a strategy. Strategy implies that your organization is taking a new and different direction. It involves choosing: selecting a course of action from among other alternatives. Strategy is the way your organization is going to change itself and change the public it seeks to serve.

When it comes to fundraising, we've come to believe that there are five fundamental strategies or major directions you can pursue. Each of these strategies offers one or more key benefits that complement and support your organization's larger mission—for example:

- Growth will complement an organization's mission that involves reaching more people.

- Involvement can support an organization whose mission is to bring about new understanding and advances in knowledge.

- Visibility is a useful strategy for a group whose mission requires making a big impact on the larger society.

- Efficiency may be a wise fundraising strategy for an organization that offers lots of direct service.

- Stability can be a beneficial strategy if an agency's mission compels it to stick around for the long haul.

Why Pursuing *One* Strategy Is Essential

After reviewing the chart of the five strategies, you might say, "Good. Makes sense to me. Our organization would really benefit from pursuing *all* of these fundraising strategies. Our programs are multifaceted, our resource development efforts are sophisticated, and we really need to make progress on all these fronts."

The premise of this book, however, is that fundraising success comes when you pick *one* fundraising strategy and pursue it with single-minded determination. In fact, we've learned that trying to focus on more than one strategy almost always leads to frustration and failure.

Here, strategy by strategy, is why we believe it's important to select one primary fundraising strategy.

Growth

If Growth is your primary strategy, then you will find it difficult, if not impossible, to:

- Devote enough time and money to foster significant donor Involvement, because Growth requires significant capital investment and because a large proportion of your donors will be newly acquired throughout your Growth phase and will thus be resistant to involvement opportunities

- Invest resources in seeking Visibility, because Growth pays more attention to acquiring large numbers of prospective donors than to cultivating the media contacts, gatekeepers, and celebrities who will help you raise your organization's public profile

- Keep fundraising costs low (Efficiency), because as you seek to add more donors, you find that most prospects don't give, those who do give make relatively smaller gifts, and the return on your investment in acquiring new donors will likely be very limited in the short run

- Achieve Stability in the short run, because your organization will be flooded with an influx of new donors whose future giving cannot be accurately predicted, and because you will have swings in income and cash flow given the high cost and large scale of donor acquisition efforts designed to accelerate Growth

Involvement

If Involvement is your primary strategy, then you will find it much more difficult to do the following:

- Grow your donor file at a rapid rate, because Involvement typically requires a bigger investment in donor file maintenance and membership or donor service efforts (thus reducing the funds available for new-donor acquisition) and because an emphasis on donor Involvement may discourage some prospective contributors who want only to send you money

- Achieve as high a public profile as you might wish, since a Visibility strategy that would help you attain that would require investing in such external activities as advertising, media, and public relations rather than in internal efforts such as membership service

- Attain the highest possible level of Efficiency because investments in Involvement are likely to raise the cost of fundraising in the short run—even though they may be conducive to greater efficiency in the long run

- Achieve short-term Stability, since the time and effort invested in fostering donor involvement may detract from efforts to cultivate major donors, promote planned giving, and emphasize the building of an endowment—all important elements in a Stability strategy

Visibility

If your primary strategy is Visibility, then you won't be able to:

- Invest the necessary resources in the donor acquisition efforts that are central to a Growth strategy

- Give overriding emphasis to donor Involvement, because Visibility requires casting the net of your outreach effort to the public at large— far beyond the limited universe of donor prospects who would want to play a role in your organization

- Achieve Efficiency in your fundraising operation, since Visibility almost by definition isn't efficient in strictly financial terms

- Pursue a course of Stability in the short term, because Visibility is typically pursued to lay the foundation for later activities that will make Stability feasible—building the organization's reputation and name recognition so that a capital campaign or planned giving promotion might be more likely to succeed

Efficiency

If your strategy is Efficiency, then it's impossible to:

- Employ an aggressive Growth strategy because Growth invariably requires a high initial investment to identify, acquire, and acknowledge all the new donors you need if you wish to grow

- Give high priority to Involvement, because that would require offering donors more than bare-bones membership or donor services, which would raise the cost of fundraising

- Seek the greatest possible Visibility, since that too would require expenditures that would reduce the Efficiency of your fundraising efforts

- Ensure maximum Stability, which requires broad diversification of your fundraising efforts, not just a concentration on those that are the most cost-efficient in the short run

Stability

If Stability is your primary fundraising strategy, your organization will be unable to:

- Pursue rapid Growth in the donor file as a top priority, which would entail significant investment that might force you to curtail other fundraising activities necessary for a fully diversified and sustainable development program

- Foster the optimal level of donor Involvement, because an Involvement strategy could destabilize other funding sources as you devote time and resources to involving donors, and you may overlook good funding sources that will support you financially but prefer not to be deeply involved in your organization

- To achieve high Visibility, which could prove to be costly and a temporary drain of the resources necessary to sustain a well-balanced fundraising program—and Visibility often entails highlighting one dimension of your organization or even seeking controversy

- Ensure maximum Efficiency, since a stable fundraising program by definition consists of a diversified range of programs, some of which are necessarily less efficient than others

You Need a *Secondary* Strategy Too

It's probably apocryphal but the great American nineteenth-century philosopher Ralph Waldo Emerson is reputed to have said, "Of course I exaggerate; that's the only way to tell the truth." To tell the truth about fundraising, we've been exaggerating our emphasis on a primary strategy; we've been saying that fundraising success comes from choosing just one strategy and sticking single-mindedly to it. Now we're going to introduce the concept of a *secondary* strategy as essential for fundraising success. You might be thinking, "What's going on here?"

The truth is that if your organization relentlessly and blindly pursued a single fundraising strategy, it would eventually destroy itself. Human behavior and group dynamics are just too complex and unpredictable for any organization do only one thing. For example, if all your fundraising program focused on was Growth at any cost, you'd soon run out of funds to bring about that Growth—and you probably would alienate some of your major funders since you no longer have time to pay attention to them. Or if you were single-mindedly efficient, you'd stop sending thank-you letters to donors. And they would stop sending you contributions.

We're recommending that your organization concentrate the allocation of its resources on one primary fundraising strategy. And the best way to ensure success is to select a secondary strategy that sets appropriate and useful limits or boundaries as you pursue your primary strategy. In a sense, the secondary strategy operates as a governing and guiding principle that supports and therefore strengthens your primary strategy.

You may recall that we have already said that a strategy is *not* how your organization gets somewhere in the future. Rather strategy is the "where" you want to be—or the direction you're headed in. It's a paradox of organizational life that to get from here to there, you have to take what seems a roundabout path. A secondary strategy isn't the only way your organization fulfills its primary fundraising strategy, but the secondary strategy does add essential discipline and direction to your pursuit of a primary strategy.

Table 4.1 will help you understand some of the principal ways in which a secondary strategy can serve in pursuit of a primary strategy.

TABLE 4.1
How Secondary Strategies Support Primary Strategies

Primary Strategy	Secondary Strategy	Relationship
Growth	Involvement	Opportunities for donor involvement increase the attractiveness of a solicitation for many donors.
	Visibility	Higher public visibility boosts response to donor acquisition efforts.
	Efficiency	Efficient fundraising frees up funds to invest in growth and appeals to many more prospects.
	Stability	A stable fundraising base permits the risk taking inherent in donor acquisition efforts.
Involvement	Growth	A growing donor base makes donor involvement activities more cost-effective.
	Visibility	Higher public visibility makes donor involvement more rewarding for participants.
	Efficiency	Greater efficiency frees up funds to invest in donor involvement activities.
	Stability	A stable and thus diverse fundraising program attracts a variety of volunteers, offers multiple opportunities for donor involvement, and makes investment in new involvement activities easier.
Visibility	Growth	A growing donor base can help promote visibility by multiplying opportunities for word-of-mouth promotion (the best advertising) and increasing the amount of volunteer energy available.
	Involvement	Donor involvement activities such as volunteer jobs promote far wider public awareness of a nonprofit's work.

(Continued)

TABLE 4.1   *(Continued)*

Primary Strategy	Secondary Strategy	Relationship
Visibility (continued)	Efficiency	An efficient fundraising program generates the funds needed to invest in visibility efforts.
	Stability	Stability enhances the capacity of a nonprofit to invest in visibility and makes the organization more credible in the eyes of the media.
Efficiency	Growth	Growth makes increased efficiencies possible by expanding the donor base and thus lowering unit costs in the donor development program.
	Involvement	Donor involvement activities boost efforts to solicit major gifts and planned gifts, as well as other highly efficient forms of donor upgrading.
	Visibility	Higher public visibility raises response (and thus lowers costs) in donor acquisition and resolicitation programs alike.
	Stability	A stable fundraising program allows a nonprofit to seek greater efficiencies by permitting the shift of resources from less efficient to more efficient fundraising programs.
Stability	Growth	Growth in the donor base is desirable when only a very minor portion of a nonprofit's revenue comes from individual donors.
	Involvement	Involvement can promote stability by enhancing chances for donors to accept new fundraising opportunities, such as major or planned gifts.
	Visibility	Visibility typically supports all fundraising programs, lending added prestige and satisfaction to donors for their gifts.
	Efficiency	Rising efficiency may increase the chances for an organization to diversify its fundraising activities by yielding the necessary capital to invest in additional fundraising activities.

Conclusion

So far, this workbook has given you the opportunity to assess the health of your organization's fundraising efforts as well as the strengths and weaknesses of the key players in those efforts. In Step Four, you've been introduced to the costs and benefits of each of the five fundamental fundraising strategies, and you have seen why choosing only *one* primary strategy and *one* secondary strategy is essential to success. Now it's time to make that selection.

Choose the Fundraising Strategy That's Right for Your Organization's Mission

YOU'RE AT THE halfway point—at the very center of this strategy-setting process. We hope this workbook has helped you to determine the state of your organization's development programs, board, and staff; to understand the value of identifying both a primary and a secondary strategy; and to recruit a team of people who are committed to coming up with practical solutions. Now it's time to pick the winner: the strategy that will help your organization raise more money to fund the valuable work you do. The exercises in this step will guide your selection of the best primary fundraising strategy, as well as a secondary strategy that will help you reach your primary strategy.

Remember that choosing one primary strategy is the wisest course for fundraising success, and selecting a secondary strategy will help you achieve your primary strategy. We'd be surprised (and a little worried) if you found this step of selecting primary and secondary fundraising strategies to be easy. On the one hand, it can get confusing as the differences among the strategies start to blur. On the other hand, it's really tempting to want your organization to pursue more than one primary fundraising strategy. They all look so good, don't they? What's not to like?

We offer three suggestions at this point:

1. Remember that you are selecting a strategy that's right *at this point in your organization's history.* We're not saying this is the one strategy you have to pursue for all time. As your organization matures and responds to circumstances, you'll almost certainly be aiming at one of the four strategies you didn't pick now.

2. Strategic planning helps organizations become more effective because it provides a rationale and time frame for concentrating the organization's scarce resources. When you pick one strategy, your organization can be determined and single-minded about that course of action—and your time, money, and energy won't be dissipated by activities unrelated to that central strategy.

3. As we explained in Step Two, each of the five strategies, in one way or another, precludes an equal emphasis on the others.

Which Primary Fundraising Strategy Is Right for Your Organization?

Exercise 5.1 will help you identify the appropriate primary fundraising strategy for your organization. Your candid and thoughtful responses to just ten questions will do the job. As you complete this exercise, keep the following considerations in mind:

- We suggest you *do not* respond to the questions based on the course you believe your organization is currently pursuing. Instead, use your own best judgment to determine the course you think would be optimal.

- You may find it challenging to make some of the choices in the exercise, but it is very important that you make those choices anyway. Setting a strategy is a matter of choosing one path rather than another. (And whoever said fundraising would be easy?)

- If you are (or think you ought to be) heavily engaged in doing A *in order to* achieve B, your strategic goal is B, not A. For instance, you may decide you need to expand your donor base—that is, to grow—in order to diversify your funding sources (perhaps to add new streams of revenue from direct mail and telephone fundraising on top of a lucrative major donor program). In that case, you are (or think you ought to be) pursuing a primary strategy of Stability, not Growth. Growth is merely a means through which you achieve greater Stability.

To complete Exercise 5.1, place a check mark in the columns to the right of the question under the letter that matches your choice: G, I, V, E, and S (corresponding, of course, to each of the five strategies in turn: Growth, Involvement, Visibility, Efficiency, and Stability). Avoid the boxes shaded gray. Use only the white boxes.

To interpret your responses in Exercise 5.1, consider the following guidelines:

- If you checked "Not Sure" for any question, think about the comparison again. Do research, if necessary. Talk to staff or trustees. To be clear about your fundraising strategy, you need to be able to answer all ten questions—and, in setting strategy, clarity is paramount.

EXERCISE 5.1

Which Fundraising Strategy Is Right for Your Organization?

Question	G	I	V	E	S	Neither Is More Important	Not Sure
(E) Is it more important for your organization to raise money at the lowest possible cost per dollar raised? Or (S) is it more important to ensure the long-term survival of your organization?	▓	▓	▓				
(E) Is it more important for your organization to raise money at the lowest possible cost per dollar raised? Or (V) is it more important for your organization to gain public visibility?	▓	▓			▓		
(E) Is it more important for your organization to raise money at the lowest possible cost per dollar raised? Or (I) is it more important for your organization to involve donors as volunteers, activists, or patrons?	▓		▓		▓		
(E) Is it more important for your organization to raise money at the lowest possible cost per dollar raised? Or (G) is it more important to increase your fundraising revenue to allow for the organization's growth?		▓	▓		▓		
(S) Is it more important for your organization to ensure its long-term survival? Or (V) is it more important for your organization to gain public visibility?	▓	▓		▓			
(S) Is it more important for your organization to ensure its long-term survival? Or (I) is it more important for your organization to involve donors as volunteers, activists, or patrons?	▓		▓	▓			
(S) Is it more important for your organization to ensure its long-term survival? Or (G) is it more important to increase your fundraising revenue to allow for the organization's growth?		▓	▓	▓			
(V) Is it more important for your organization to gain public visibility? Or (I) is it more important for your organization to involve donors as volunteers, activists, or patrons?	▓			▓	▓		
(V) Is it more important for your organization to gain public visibility? Or (G) is it more important to increase your fundraising revenue to allow for the organization's growth?		▓		▓	▓		
(I) Is it more important for your organization to involve donors as volunteers, activists, or patrons? Or (G) is it more important to increase your fundraising revenue to allow for the organization's growth?			▓	▓	▓		
SCORE							

TABLE 5.1

Interpreting Your Score in Exercise 5.1

Letter checks

3 + times	Interpretation
G	Your primary goal is GROWTH whether in increased revenue or in the number of your donors or members. Your development program will be shaped by the demands (and the costs) of sustaining a high rate of growth.
I	Donor INVOLVEMENT is central to your organization's mission. Your work requires broad-based participation in volunteer activities, grassroots lobbying, or merchandise sales—or you must have attendance at performances or other events. Your fundraising efforts ought to be reviewed for the opportunities they provide for donors to be involved in the organization's affairs.
V	Your mission requires broad-based public support, which you can only achieve through VISIBILITY. Your fundraising program needs to be designed to help you gain public attention—and executed in ways that are consistent with the image your work requires.
E	The hallmark of your fundraising stragtegy is EFFICIENCY. The preponderance of your fundraising activities need to be focused on raising money at the lowest possible cost-per-dollar-raised.
S	STABILITY is the key to your development strategy. Most of your effort and creativity ought to zero in on ways to ensure your organization's long-term survival.

- If you checked "Neither Is More Important" more than twice, you may have a problem making decisions. To establish clear goals, every nonprofit needs to set priorities in all of these critical areas. Think it through again!

- If you answered at least nine of the ten questions, then count the number of times you selected each letter (A through E) as more important.

Use Table 5.1 to evaluate your score.

Which Secondary Fundraising Strategy Is Right for Your Organization?

Turn next to Exercise 5.2, which consists of five parts that will help you select a secondary strategy. Remember that the secondary strategy provides limits or boundaries to help you pursue your primary fundraising strategy—and to do so in a way that recognizes the unique needs and opportunities your organization faces. Your secondary strategy complements and supports the chief strategy. You need to complete only the one part of Exercise 5.2 that corresponds to your primary strategy.

In Exercise 5.2, rank from a *high* score of 1 to a *low* score of 4 the relative value of each available secondary strategy that corresponds to the primary strategy you've chosen. The secondary strategy that is ranked 1 is the one that will best complement your primary strategy. Ideally, no two secondary

---

EXERCISE 5.2

Choosing Your Secondary Fundraising Strategy

	Rank (1, high, to 4, low)
If your primary strategy is GROWTH, what is the biggest obstacle you face in pursuing that strategy?	

- Is a lack of *Involvement* opportunities for donors limiting the number of those who will support your organization? _____
- Is a lack of public *Visibility* making it difficult for you to acquire lots of new donors? _____
- Is the lack of *Efficiency* in your donor development program making it uneconomic for you to recruit new donors? _____
- Is the lack of reliable and diverse funding sources (that is, *Stability*) denying you the capital you need to prospect for new donors? _____

	Rank
If your primary strategy is INVOLVEMENT, what is the biggest obstacle you face in pursuing that strategy?	

- Is a lack of *Growth* in your donor base making it difficult to expand donor involvement activities, because there aren't enough donors to do that cost-effectively? _____
- Is a lack of public *Visibility* making it difficult for you to persuade donors that *Involvement* is important and rewarding? _____
- Is the absence of an *Efficient* donor development program denying you the funds you need to offer more donor *Involvement* activities? _____
- Is the lack of reliable and diverse funding sources (that is, *Stability*) making it too risky for you to spend time and money offering opportunities for *Involvement* on the part of your donors? _____

	Rank
If your primary strategy is VISIBILITY, what is the biggest obstacle you face in pursuing that strategy?	

- Is a lack of *Growth* in your donor base limiting your access to volunteers to help promote your organization? _____
- Is a lack of *Involvement* activities for donors limiting your opportunities to generate word-of–mouth promotion? _____
- Is the *Efficiency* of your donor development program already so low (in other words, are you so inefficient) that you can't afford to spend money (and raise your cost ratio further) to promote your organization's *Visibility*? _____
- Is the lack of reliable and diverse funding sources (that is, *Stability*) denying you the capital you need to invest in *Visibility,* or even to persuade the public that your organization is worthy of notice? _____

	Rank
If your primary strategy is EFFICIENCY, what is the biggest obstacle you face in pursuing that strategy?	

- Has a lack of *Growth* in your donor base limited the number of your donors, to the point that your donor development activities are not cost-effective? _____
- Is a lack of *Involvement* activities for donors reducing their interest in low-cost, highly efficient forms of fundraising such as major or planned gifts? _____
- Is the lack of *Visibility* hampering your efforts to raise funds from major donors or institutional sources such as foundations or corporations? _____
- Is the lack of reliable and diverse funding sources (that is, *Stability*) preventing you from focusing single-mindedly on increasing the *Efficiency* of your donor development program? _____

(Continued)

EXERCISE 5.2   (Continued)

If your primary strategy is STABILITY, what is the biggest obstacle you face in pursuing that strategy?	Rank
• Does a lack of *Growth* in your donor base mean that you have too few donors to provide breadth and reliability to your fundraising program?	_____
• Is a lack of *Involvement* activities for donors unduly limiting your opportunities to cultivate and upgrade your donors?	_____
• Is the lack of *Visibility* hampering your efforts to attract funding from a variety of sources and thus broaden your fundraising base?	_____
• Is the lack of *Efficiency* in your donor development program denying you the funds you need to diversify your fundraising efforts?	_____

---

strategies will have the same rank for any given primary strategy. But life isn't always that simple. Your best intentions notwithstanding, you might find yourself staring at two—or even three—1s or 2s. If that's the case, it's important that you select just one secondary strategy. Here are two tips to help you in case of such indecision:

- After comparing notes, ask the members of your strategy team to repeat the exercise. Once informed by the views of other members, they might come up with different answers.

- If simply discussing and repeating Exercise 5.2 doesn't do the trick, pose a couple of tough questions to be applied to each of the top secondary strategies, and try once again. Ask such things as, "Do we have the necessary resources [staff, funding, consultants] to pursue this secondary strategy?" and "Is this secondary strategy the most advantageous course for us to pursue *at this time*?"

Eventually, you'll arrive at a consensus if you doggedly work at that approach. We encourage you to take time to put your primary and secondary strategies in writing and to list the three key reasons you believe those are the best strategies for your organization at this time in its history.

Conclusion

Now you have a solid sense of both the primary and the secondary fundraising strategies that are ideally suited for your organization at this stage in its existence. To put that strategy to work for your organization, the next step is to set goals. Step Six will usher you through that process.

Step Six

Set Fundraising Goals That Support Your Fundraising Strategy

BOTH INFORMAL conversations and formal research confirm that the desire to support an organization's mission is the most important factor in motivating donors to provide financial support. That's why we believe that your mission must be the primary factor in your fundraising strategy.

This workbook is designed to help you pick the strategy that reinforces and complements your organization's mission. In other words, the strategy you selected in the previous step should help your current and prospective donors see how their contributions support the realization of your organization's mission. But the strategy you selected will lead to success only if you take the next step of coming up with goals to implement it. Without meaningful goals, your strategy will be nothing more than an abstract concept.

Optimistic Goals and Realistic Objectives

When it comes to setting goals, many organizations find themselves derailed in their planning process. We've watched nonprofit boards of directors as well as both staff and volunteer committees get mired down in the great argument between the Optimists and the Pessimists (sometimes portrayed as the Visionaries and the Pragmatists). One side is always coming up with wild ideas and totally unrealistic goals, while the other side argues these ideas or goals can't be implemented or achieved. The visionaries want to grow and expand, to serve new markets and offer new services, while the pragmatists know from experience that those new initiatives must be supported financially and that if you reach too far in life, you can slip and fall.

We think this great debate is misplaced. When it comes to nonprofit fundraising, it's not an either-or proposition. In our view, the problem is that boards and committees often confuse goals and objectives. To succeed, your organization needs both: big, audacious goals that set the course for the next several years, *as well as* achievable and measurable objectives that will closely shape your work on a monthly and quarterly basis. The objectives state what will actually be achieved or in place within a specific period of time, and those achievements represent some real progress toward your organization's more distant goals.

We can't emphasize enough that you need *both* goals and objectives. The following two paragraphs are central to our argument; read them *carefully*.

Without goals, you'll be tempted to start up a bunch of fundraising programs that "feel right" to you or that you guess you can manage adequately. But you'll almost surely have trouble attracting and keeping donors, because they won't see the connection between their financial support and the mission they care about. And you need goals that are unrealistic because—even though you will probably never achieve them—you'll get further along by pursuing those ambitious goals. Setting the bar a little higher each time around will stretch your organization's staff and volunteers.

Without objectives, these ambitious goals are meaningless because objectives are how goals are translated into real work with real donors and prospects. The pragmatists among our readers will be pleased that we've devoted the entire next chapter to objectives.

How to Set Audacious Goals

For this step, we've provided five exercises, each one designed to help you set goals for one of each of five fundraising strategies. We encourage you to take a stab at all of the exercises—even those for fundraising strategies you didn't select. This will serve as a double-check to make sure that you did indeed pick the best possible primary and secondary strategies—or that you selected a *new* strategy if you are using this workbook to reevaluate the strategy you chose several years ago.

As you complete these exercises, you'll notice that the questions are different for each strategy—further evidence that the strategy you choose has important implications and that pursuing more than one primary strategy inevitably involves you in pursuing conflicting and contradictory goals.

To work your way through these exercises, you'll need to use your imagination. At this stage in the planning process, you're imagining what the future will be like for your organization. If what you conceive as a goal can be put in place this year, it's probably not a goal. Setting goals helps you envision what will characterize your organization's fundraising efforts over the long term.

For example, if your primary strategy is Growth with a secondary strategy of Involvement, one of your goals might be to launch a monthly lecture series that involves at least half of your donors. It would be a rare organization that could pull off this feat in a single year. And if you have any experience in fundraising, you know that doing anything on a monthly basis and that attracting "at least half of your donors" make this an audacious goal.

This example also illustrates the difference between goals and objectives. You want to end up with a monthly lecture series, but to get there you'll have to articulate some very specific objectives. For instance, an objective might be: "Within the next three months, identify six experienced staff members who are capable of presenting stimulating lectures, and persuade them to participate."

We'll talk more about setting objectives in Step Seven. Here, we are urging you to set fundraising goals that are bigger and longer term than is usually the case when staff and volunteers sit down to do planning. We encourage you to act as though there aren't any right answers—that your organization has all the money it needs, the best possible staff, and talented volunteers with lots of time. In short, don't worry about being realistic.

To illustrate how different goals can fulfill a particular strategy, Table 6.1 gives three examples of goals for each of the five fundraising strategies. We hope you'll use your imagination and adapt these examples to your organization.

Now it's time for you and your strategy planning team to develop goals to carry out your primary fundraising strategy. Exercises 6.1 through 6.5 will guide you in that endeavor.

You and your strategy team could spend hours—and many meetings—discussing all these goals. And you could use elaborate group process techniques to tabulate and finally agree on the goals that your committee or task force wants. But our suggestion is that after a relatively brief discussion, you repeat this process for your organization's secondary strategy. Use the CD-ROM or photocopy a second set of exercise sheets so you can complete these five exercises for five different secondary strategies.

Remember that the *secondary* strategy you selected in Step Five is the planning tool that helps you set limits or boundaries on your primary strategy. Without these constraints, your fundraising program could become too unbalanced. Put more positively, the secondary strategy complements and completes your primary strategy. Thus, the process of drafting goals for your secondary strategy will help you examine the goals for your primary strategy from a new perspective. With this added insight, you may want to

---

TABLE 6.1

Examples of Audacious Goals to Support Your Organization's Fundraising Strategy

Your Primary Strategy Is Growth

- Double the size of our membership within three years
- Increase by 20 percent the number of donors making annual gifts of $5,000 or more
- Secure 50 percent more income from parents of children involved in our programs

Your Primary Strategy Is Involvement

- Recruit 10 percent of our membership to participate in three new annual giving societies
- Have at least three major donors visit our facilities every month of the year
- Revamp the 800 telephone number and Web site to provide donors with twenty-four-hour, user-friendly avenues for requesting information, ordering materials, and enrolling for educational opportunities

Your Primary Strategy Is Visibility

- Establish broad-based and substantive relationships with the editorial board and top feature writers of the local newspaper
- Refocus and reconfigure all volunteer opportunities to attract television coverage
- Recruit an advisory council of outstanding experts who are also willing to speak on behalf of the organization

Your Primary Strategy Is Efficiency

- Take our income-to-cost ratio from 2:2 to 3:1, so that for every dollar spent in fundraising, we receive at least three dollars
- Abandon every special event that is unprofitable three years in a row
- Double the percentage of our overall income received from major donors

Your Primary Strategy Is Stability

- Ensure that no one funding source is responsible for more than 25 percent of the annual budget
- Launch a monthly giving program that provides at least 10 percent of our organization's annual budget within five years
- Have at least 25 percent of our income secured by multiyear commitments from major donors

---

modify one or more of your goals so they more fully support your primary strategy.

At this point, your strategy team should review all of your goals and then select the top three to five goals. Take time to write out these goals; a rough draft is fine—don't get caught up in wordsmithing. Select those goals you believe most strongly reflect the primary strategy you've chosen. Strategic planning is about making choices; having too many goals will dissipate your organization's time and resources.

EXERCISE 6.1

Setting Goals for Growth

If your organization's primary fundraising strategy is to increase its donor base, that is, Growth, what would need to be true about your development program at the end of three years?

Number of donors or members: _____

Average gift per member or donor: _____

Number of major donors: _____

Total amount contributed each year by major donors: _____

Total amount of contributed income: _____

Number of foundation grants received: _____

Total amount of foundation grants: _____

Number of corporate gifts received: _____

Total amount of corporate gifts received: _____

Number of bequest or planned giving donors enrolled in heritage or legacy society: _____

EXERCISE 6.2

Setting Goals for Involvement

1. **If your primary fundraising strategy is to Involve your donors or members, what involvement opportunities or activities would exist at the end of three years?**

    For those making modest contributions:

    a. _____

    b. _____

    c. _____

    For those making major contributions:

    a. _____

    b. _____

    c. _____

    For foundations and institutional donors:

    a. _____

    b. _____

    c. _____

2. **What other involvement activities might your organization initiate for some or all of your donors?**

    Letter writing or communicating with staff:

    a. _____

    b. _____

    c. _____

    Visits or tours of your facilities:

    a. _____

    b. _____

    c. _____

    Educational events, if any:

    a. _____

    b. _____

    c. _____

    Social events, if any:

    a. _____

    b. _____

    c. _____

    Distribution of publications or resource materials:

    a. _____

    b. _____

    c. _____

EXERCISE 6.3

Setting Goals for Visibility

If your primary strategy is Visibility, what would be the character of your fundraising programs at the end of three years?

Who would now be aware of your organization's work?

a. _____

b. _____

c. _____

d. _____

What media outlets would regularly report your activities?

a. _____

b. _____

c. _____

d. _____

How widespread would be the scope of awareness?

How would the public characterize or perceive your organization?

What overall concern, specific activity, valuable service, or even tangible item would the public immediately associate with your organization?

EXERCISE 6.4

Setting Goals for Efficiency

If Efficiency is your primary strategy, what would be different about your development program at the end of three years?

Areas of concentration:

a. _____

b. _____

c. _____

d. _____

What low-response, high-cost fundraising efforts would no longer exist as a result of your focus on efficiency?

a. _____

b. _____

c. _____

d. _____

What will be the ratio of income to your fundraising expense? _____

How will funders and donors learn about your increased efficiency?

a. _____

b. _____

c. _____

d. _____

EXERCISE 6.5

Setting Goals for Stability

If you want to bring Stability to your organization's development program, what will be true about your development plan at the end of three years?

Amount of financial reserves in place? $_____

What three new or additional major sources of income will you have?

a. _____

b. _____

c. _____

What factor or factors will encourage donors or funders to continue and sustain their financial support over the long term?

a. _____

b. _____

c. _____

Which of the following fundraising programs will be instituted or more heavily emphasized, and what proportion of your overall fundraising or development effort will be devoted to each?

❑ Endowment; percentage of overall development effort: _____

❑ Planned giving; percentage of overall effort: _____

❑ Monthly giving (including electronic funds transfer); percentage of overall effort: _____

What else about your development programs will be in place to help offset the inevitable ups and downs of giving by major donors and foundations?

What will be different about your relationship with the donor or funder who is currently your organization's primary source of income?

Conclusion

After you've made those difficult choices, you're ready to go on to Step Seven, where you'll turn those big, audacious goals into specific objectives that can be measured and achieved within a specific time period.

Turn Fundraising Goals into Achievable Objectives

AT THIS STAGE, you and your strategy team have hammered out many difficult decisions. You've made some tough choices with the realization that your success depends on concentrating on one strategy—even though that means consciously excluding other attractive strategies. You've also discovered how a secondary strategy will help you achieve your primary strategy. And in Step Six, you articulated some ambitious goals that you believe will point your organization in the direction indicated by the strategy you've chosen.

It may now be time for your strategy team to sit out the next couple of innings. Specifically, it may be inappropriate and unwise for your decision-making group to go through Step Seven of setting objectives and Step Eight of selecting fundraising tactics to achieve those objectives. That's especially the case if you're involved in a larger organization with several staff in its development office. Or if your strategy team includes lots of board members or committee members.

The board of directors of any nonprofit organization sets policy—the mission, the primary direction, and major goals. Then, if there are staff, the board holds the president or executive director responsible for crafting objectives that fulfill those goals and for seeing that those objectives are indeed carried out. In Step Eight, we'll see how selecting the right tactics or techniques is essential if you're to achieve your objectives.

However, a wise executive director and a diligent development director will make sure those objectives—sometimes called work plans—are available for any board member to review. Savvy nonprofit executives may even solicit advice from individual board members who have expertise or connections that might be useful in carrying out those objectives. But objectives are primarily the staff's responsibilities.

So whether you're a staff person with the responsibility of setting objectives or a board member charged with evaluating them, you'll want to know how to lay out objectives that fulfill your organization's fundraising goals. You'll also want to make sure those goals and objectives support your primary and secondary fundraising strategies.

Why Objectives Must Be Realistic

Let's review what makes an objective different from a goal. In Step Six, we suggested that goals are ambitious (perhaps even unrealistic) targets that stretch your organization to make progress in broad areas. A good litmus test for goals is that if you can envision your organization fulfilling that goal this year, it's probably *not* a goal. It may indeed be an objective, and you should be asking yourself whether meeting that objective takes your organization toward a larger goal. In other words, an objective is achievable within a specific time frame. In most cases, the objective should include specific numbers or units that can be measured or counted. A good objective is quantifiable. You or development staff should strive to describe the objective in a precise or tangible manner. You should be able to picture a completed objective in your mind's eye.

Although an objective is realistic and specific, it is *not* yet *how* you are going to realize your results. The process or the steps you take to achieve an objective are the subject of Step Eight, where we explore fundraising tactics or methods. Those tactics are the tools you'll use to achieve or complete your measurable objectives.

Another important point is that the ambitious goals you set in Step Six are likely to require *more than one objective* if you're to make any real progress. In fact, there might be as many as three to five objectives for each goal. However, if you end up with more than five objectives, you should probably reconsider the goal you set. It may be two or three goals masquerading as a single one.

Let's look at five examples of objectives that meet goals that have grown out of an organization's strategy:

- Example One: Your primary strategy is Growth through a secondary strategy of Visibility. A *goal* of making your organization a household word in your community might involve setting an *objective* that by year's end, there will have been four feature-length articles about your organization in both of your community's major newspapers.

- Example Two: Your primary strategy is Involvement through a secondary strategy of Growth. You might set a *goal* of doubling the number of donors involved in your annual giving clubs, which would suggest an *objective* of establishing two new giving club levels by the end of this fiscal year.

- Example Three: Your primary strategy is Visibility with a secondary strategy of Involvement. You could set a *goal* of recruiting a board that includes the prominent philanthropists in your community by having as your *objective* the completion within the next six months of biographical research on at least ten philanthropists in your community.

- Example Four: Your primary strategy is Efficiency through a secondary strategy of Stability. You may want a *goal* of having no single funding source contribute more than 15 percent of your annual income, which could be realized in part with an *objective* to meet with at least one new foundation officer every month of the year.

- Example Five: You may want to pursue Stability through a secondary strategy of Efficiency. You might set a *goal* of halving the percentage of your budget spent on fundraising by laying out an *objective* of contacting twelve retail stores in the next three months to seek in-kind gifts to support your annual donor event.

As you can see, each of these objectives takes place within a limited time frame ("by year's end," "within three months"), they are tangible and precise ("feature-length articles," "biographical research"), and they can be measured and counted ("four articles in both newspapers," "twelve retail stores").

It doesn't take a genius to see that even if you achieve your objectives, you still won't have realized your goal. It will take several objectives to make a meaningful dent in the challenge you've given yourself, and you'll have to spend a number of years setting those objectives and carrying them out.

To use Example One, you may want to set a second objective of establishing a media advisory committee of at least six members who will have their first meeting no later than six months from now. Then next year, you may set an objective to create a task force of at least three persons who will meet at least twice a year with the editorial boards of your newspapers.

As you or your development staff get immersed in this objective-setting process, it's easy to lose sight of your primary strategy. In fact, having the strategy planning team review a development staff's objectives can help make sure those objectives ultimately contribute toward your primary strategy. In other words, an objective fails to support your primary strategy if it—even unintentionally—takes your organization in another direction, toward another strategy.

To use our first example where Growth is the primary strategy; an objective of twelve front-page stories about your organization's expertise could involve so much time spent cultivating media contacts that getting newspaper coverage could become an end in itself. In a real sense, Involvement has become a secondary strategy toward a primary strategy of Visibility. In that event, you won't have the time and resources left to achieve your primary strategy of Growth.

How to Set Your Objectives

Exercise 7.1 will help you set objectives that fulfill the goals you set in Step Six. We encourage you to articulate at least *three objectives for each goal,* and we hope that—if you followed our advice in Step Six and set at least five goals toward your primary and secondary strategies—you'll repeat this process for each of the goals you set in Step Six.

Exercise 7.1 is a template to use for objective setting. Copy however many you need. Then simply fill in the appropriate numbers for each goal and objective.

Conclusion

You've now set your organization's strategy, goals, and objectives. You may want to take time to put those three pieces together as a written document either in outline form or as a chart.

With this solid foundation of planning, it's now time to consider the fundraising techniques or tactics that will be most appropriate to execute your strategy. Step Eight will walk you through some of the most challenging aspects of that process.

EXERCISE 7.1

Template for Objective Setting

PRIMARY STRATEGY _____

SECONDARY STRATEGY _____

GOAL _____ (from Step Six): _____

_____

_____

OBJECTIVE _____ :

Number or units involved or size: _____

Precise, tangible description:

_____

When will you complete this objective? What is your deadline? (If it's longer than a year, go back and break this objective in smaller pieces.)

_____

How will you measure this objective? How will you know you've achieved it?

_____

How will achieving this objective bring you closer to your goal?

_____

Does your organization have the resources to achieve this objective within this time frame? If not, what additional resources will you need? (If you don't have the resources, you may need to go back and reevaluate your goal and your strategy.)

_____

How much staff time (hours or days) will be required to carry out this objective? (If your estimate is too high, you may have lost sight of your primary and secondary strategies, and this objective has become an end in itself. Remember that you set goals and objectives to get your fundraising program from where it is now to a new, strategically desirable place.)

Choose the Right Tactics for Your Fundraising Strategy and Goals

THE GOOD NEWS for nonprofit organizations is that achieving success in fundraising doesn't require superhuman intelligence. The bad news is that it usually takes lots of hard work. To undertake this hard work, you need to use the fundraising tools—individual techniques, methods, or tactics—best suited to your organization's fundraising strategy.

By this point, your fundraising planning team has selected primary and secondary strategies that complement your organization's mission. You've set some ambitious goals, and you—or, more likely, your organization's development staff—have articulated some specific objectives that will go at least partway to meeting those goals. You might want to think of these objectives as targets you want to achieve within a prescribed period of time.

To hit these targets, you'll need to use fundraising methods or engage in development activities that will produce those results. Here in Step Eight, we help you select the right tactics or fundraising methods to use in achieving these objectives or to reevaluate the tactics you're already using.

In Step Seven, we suggested that setting objectives was the province of an agency's professional staff; boards of directors establish broad policy and goals, while professional staff are held accountable for implementation as they create and manage objectives. Here at Step Eight, fundraising tactics are even more the business of staff. Indeed, large organizations have individuals who specialize in each of the tactics we discuss. Some nonprofits even have entire departments devoted to individual development tools.

This is the longest chapter in this workbook. Even though development staff will be best able to complete the exercises, we encourage *all readers* to peruse Step Eight. Even if you don't have enough information to answer the questions, spend twenty to thirty minutes reading the introductions to each subsection as well as the commentaries offered as part of the exercises. You'll be introduced to the key factors at work in fundraising tools that your organization is most likely to use.

Before you tackle the exercises in this chapter, take a few minutes to review Tables 8.1 through 8.5. These tables suggest factors to consider as

---

TABLE 8.1

Potential Applications of Fundraising Tactics to Promote Growth

Tactic	Applications in a Typical Growth Strategy
Foundation grants	If available, may support capacity building. Foundation giving does not itself support Growth.
Corporate giving	If available, may support capacity building. Corporate giving itself does not support Growth, except in cases where members or constituents are corporations.
Major gifts	Almost always attractive but usually have little to do with Growth.
Capital campaign	May require Growth to build a base of campaign prospects. Often a capital campaign is a useful Growth vehicle.
Planned giving	Encouraging bequests and other forms of planned giving may make eminently good sense but are not a likely vehicle to realize Growth.
Direct mail	Traditionally the centerpiece of a Growth strategy, used both to recruit new members or donors and to cultivate, educate, and resolicit them.
Telephone fundraising	A risky approach to Growth (donors acquired by telephone usually require expensive subsequent telephoning to renew), but can be extremely useful in specialized applications in coordination with direct mail.
Web site	An attractive way to increase Growth in membership or a donor base.
Special events	Sometimes useful for local and regional organizations as a means to recruit new donors (with the risk that donors' motives for giving may be mixed and thus a poor predictor of future behavior).
Merchandising	In direct marketing programs—mail, telephone, and Internet—often helpful as a source of premiums (membership incentives). In itself, doesn't directly support growth.

you apply any of ten commonly used fundraising tactics to pursue a particular strategy:

- Foundation grants
- Corporate giving
- Major gifts
- Capital campaign
- Planned giving

TABLE 8.2

Potential Applications of Fundraising Tactics to Promote Involvement

Tactic	Applications in a Typical Involvement Strategy
Foundation grants	Except as a possible source of funding for new programs, not often directly applicable to donor or member Involvement.
Corporate giving	Except as a possible source of funding for new programs, not often directly applicable to donor or member Involvement.
Major gifts	Personal notes and telephone calls, face-to-face solicitation, intimate major donor events, and other involving activities are frequently important in a donor Involvement strategy.
Capital campaign	Usually, heavy donor (volunteer) Involvement is useful—and often indispensable—in a capital campaign. The converse isn't necessarily true, though; a capital campaign may actually distract donors from other forms of Involvement.
Planned giving	Except as a possible source of funding for new programs, not often directly applicable to donor or member Involvement. (Encouraging planned gifts is an inherently involving activity, however.)
Direct mail	For a large or widely scattered membership or donor base, communications (both solicitations and newsletters) can encourage direct donor action and feedback.
Telephone fundraising	For a large or widely scattered membership or donor base, may be extremely useful if telephone calls encourage direct donor action and feedback— perhaps soliciting opinions as well as gifts.
Web site	Will increasingly prove to be a valuable adjunct to any Involvement strategy. Offers endless opportunities for participation and two-way communications— that is, direct donor Involvement—at extremely low cost.
Special events	May be particularly useful as a donor benefit or special gift acknowledgment. Volunteer-run events may encourage deeper Involvement.
Merchandising	Merchandise "involves" donors or members only if it affords opportunities for them to pursue efforts that support the organization's mission.

- Direct mail

- Telephone fundraising

- Web site

- Special events

- Merchandising

As you review these five tables, don't worry if you feel confused. Fundraising seeks to adapt to the full range of human interests and behaviors, so the number of fundraising tools can seem almost endless. And often there isn't any real distinction between a fundraising method and the source of income that method seeks to secure. For example, lots of nonprofit organizations have lines on their income budget that correspond to "special events" or "foundation grants." Special events and foundations

---

TABLE 8.3

Potential Applications of Fundraising Tactics to Promote Visibility

Tactic	Applications in a Typical Visibility Strategy
Foundation grants	Except as a possible source of funding for new attention-getting efforts, not often directly applicable to Visibility.
Corporate giving	Except as a possible source of funding for new attention-getting efforts, not often directly applicable to Visibility.
Major gifts	Except as a possible source of funding for new attention-getting efforts, not often directly applicable to Visibility.
Capital campaign	Visibility may be the centerpiece of a capital campaign's public phase. And a capital campaign, especially with highly visible bricks-and-mortar products, may be useful to focus attention-getting efforts.
Planned giving	Except as a possible source of funding for new attention-getting efforts, not often directly applicable to Visibility.
Direct mail	Often expensive though potentially effective means to gain Visibility. Requires added capital to fund attention-getting mail that doesn't necessarily bring in lots of gifts.
Telephone fundraising	Because of its high cost per contact, not often useful to gain Visibility.
Web site	An excellent tool for Internet-based promotional efforts.
Special events	Frequently very useful to spotlight an organization or a campaign, especially with celebrity support.
Merchandising	May help gain Visibility through such means as decals, calendars, mugs, and T–shirts.

TABLE 8.4

Potential Applications of Fundraising Tactics to Promote Efficiency

Tactic	Applications in a Typical Efficiency Strategy
Foundation grants	All fundraising from institutions tends to be (or ought to be) highly Efficient.
Corporate giving	All fundraising from institutions tends to be (or ought to be) highly Efficient.
Major gifts	Often a very Efficient way to lower the cost of fundraising.
Capital campaign	By offering donors incentives to give larger gifts, may be especially useful in gaining Efficiency.
Planned giving	In the long run, where planned giving is applicable, is typically the most Efficient form of fundraising.
Direct mail	Usually not very Efficient, though there are exceptions, such as monthly sustainer programs and high-dollar-giving clubs.
Telephone fundraising	A high-cost fundraising technique. Promotes Efficiency only in supporting a monthly sustainer program or high-dollar-giving club.
Web site	Potentially very Efficient. Usually requires up-front investment, however.
Special events	Rarely Efficient.
Merchandising	Typically, a low-margin (and therefore inefficient) activity.

are indeed sources of income, but to realize that income organizations must use fundraising tools that are called "event fundraising" or "grant writing." If you stick with it long enough, it will all make sense (or perhaps you'll realize that it doesn't make sense, but that doesn't really matter either!).

Step Eight will help you evaluate in greater depth the potential uses of five fundraising tactics. Your organization may be using other development tools, and when it comes to generating revenue for nonprofits, there are certainly many other methods. But in our experience, these five are the most commonly used. They also serve as a foundation for adding more sophisticated development initiatives. If you're not using these basic tools, the exercises will help you consider adding them to your development program. If you're already using these tools, the exercises offer you insights about how your organization might improve its use of these popular fundraising tactics.

Once you've completed exercises for each of these tactics, you'll want to take a stab at the sixth exercise. Or, more likely, you will encourage your development staff to carry out this step and report back to you. This sixth

TABLE 8.5

Potential Applications of Fundraising Tactics to Promote Stability

Tactic	Applications in a Typical Stability Strategy
Foundation grants	Very useful as part of a diversified, broad-based fundraising program designed to gain or sustain Stability.
Corporate giving	Very useful as part of a diversified, broad-based fundraising program designed to gain or sustain Stability.
Major gifts	Almost always an indispensable part of the mix when seeking Stability.
Capital campaign	Very useful as part of a diversified, broad-based fundraising program designed to gain or sustain Stability.
Planned giving	Almost always an indispensable part of the mix when seeking Stability.
Direct mail	Useful in gaining Stability only as a means to diversify by building an individual membership or donor base where that's lacking or to launch other efforts to diversify (such as through monthly giving or a high-dollar club).
Telephone fundraising	Useful in gaining Stability only as a means to diversify by building an individual membership or donor base where that's lacking or to launch other efforts to diversify (such as through monthly giving or a high-dollar club).
Web site	Almost always an indispensable part of the mix when seeking Stability, which requires maximizing efforts to communicate with donors or members.
Special events	Can be useful as donor-acknowledgment or donor-participation activities—not necessarily as a means to raise net cash and thus not essential to maintaining Stability.
Merchandising	Irrelevant to a Stability strategy, except where merchandise helps to strengthen donor or member relationships.

exercise will help you decide which of the five tactics to use to achieve the objectives you set in Step Seven.

Capital Campaigns

Capital campaigns have traditionally been used to build buildings or endowment funds (or both). Increasingly, though, nonprofits include funds for maintenance, staffing, or special programs in their campaign goals. It's no secret why. The hoopla and the intensity of a capital campaign frequently move donors to dig far more deeply into their pockets than they do for annual fund appeals or other workaday solicitations. During capital campaigns, donors will sometimes give gifts ten times as large as they usually do.

There's something very special about a capital campaign: genuine excitement and energy, lots of volunteer involvement, and often great success. Regrettably, though, capital campaigns also require special conditions and extensive preparations. Completing Exercise 8.1 will give you a preliminary indication as to whether it's worthwhile for your organization to explore in depth a possible campaign.

This exercise will also help you evaluate your organization's capacity for securing major gifts, whether for your ongoing operations (sometimes called an annual fund) or to underwrite a special program. Major gift fundraising works best when it's organized as a campaign. In many cases, the chief difference between a major gifts drive and a capital campaign is duration. Capital campaign pledges are typically fulfilled over a period of three to five years, while most major gifts programs are seeking gifts for the current year.

It's not enough to get a passing grade on this self-test as adequate proof that your organization is ready to launch a capital campaign. If you get a green light from this exercise, you should then hire a firm or individual experienced in conducting feasibility studies (or precampaign assessment). The stakes are high in capital campaigns. Failure can be more than costly; it can destroy an organization. Completing this exercise will help you decide whether it even makes sense to take the next step of carrying out a feasibility study.

This instrument measures twenty independent criteria of an organization's readiness for a capital campaign. Separately, each of the measures is significant. Together, at the right levels and in the proper combination, they ensure the success of a capital program.

Exercise 8.1 is most effective when completed individually by board members and then discussed in a group session. A candid and thorough discussion of each item will help the strategy planning team come to a complete understanding of the pros and cons of a capital campaign. You'll also be able to identify specific next steps to take if you're interested in using a capital campaign as one of the techniques to achieve your fundraising objectives.

The "Score" column calls for your subjective rating; 10 is the highest score, 1 the lowest. If you believe your organization deserves a top rating, then give the item a 10. If you think there's room for improvement, make an assessment of how serious the deficiency is, and determine the rating. Each item in this exercise is given a weight (see the explanation at the top of Exercise 8.1.). The higher the weight is, the greater is the consequence of the criterion for the success of the campaign. Each has been measured carefully for its significance.

Multiply your rating in the "Score" column times the weight given, and indicate the total in the third column. When you're finished, total the third column. To interpret your score, see Table 8.6.

EXERCISE 8.1

Is Your Organization Ready for a Capital Campaign or a Major Gift Drive?

Use the following weights to score each item in the exercise:

Score	Meaning
10	Best possible rating
9	Excellent, but not perfect
8	Very good, but requires some attention
7	Good, but needs improvement
6	Satisfactory, but not good enough to do the job
5	Less than satisfactory; needs serious work
4 or less	Unacceptable; immediate correction called for

Factor	Score	Weight	Total
1. During the past 12 months, you've operated under a written plan to actively cultivate your top 200 sources, and you've made a significant contact with each of them at least twice during the year. It's not good enough to just have the list. You need to be in contact with these sources, romancing your cause and your case. Give yourself a "10" if you have an active and effective program of prospect management and cultivation.		× 5 =	
2. The board and staff have individually committed in an open meeting, with full discussion and open voting, their dedication to give and work sacrificially. A capital campaign starts with the board and staff. If those on the side don't care, why should anyone else?		× 4 =	
3. The board as a group is able to give 10% of the campaign objective. There have been many successful campaigns where the board is not able to give this much. But if they are able to give 10% or better, it helps ensure a victory for the campaign. If you believe board members will be able to give 15% of the campaign objective, give yourself a rating of "10." Ten percent of the giving should be a "9." Anything lower than 10% should be evaluated accordingly.		× 4 =	
4. You are able to determine or identify the 20 major gifts that will produce 40% of your objective. The campaign cannot be successful without major gifts. If within your donor constituency there isn't the potential to give 40% of your objective in 20 large gifts, your campaign is very likely moribund. And if you can't identify these sources, you haven't started the campaign process. Give yourself a "10" if you have isolated these 20 sources. (If you're able to generate 40% of your objective with fewer than 20 sources, all the better!)		× 3 =	

Factor	Score	Weight	Total
5. There is wholehearted agreement between the staff and board that this is a worthy project, and they are willing to work together to bring the project to fruition. It's not uncommon for staff to initiate ideas and often to be the inspiration behind a campaign project. You hope to have a staff that provides leadership and motivation. But it is unacceptable to have a capital program entirely staff-driven. There must be a sharing of vision and dreams. The board must accept the project as their own. Give yourself a "10" if there is total and wholehearted agreement, and a sense of excitement and high expectations. If this doesn't exist, or if some board members aren't enthusiastic advocates of the project, give yourself less than a "10". The situation needs to be corrected—or the apathetic (or negative) directors need to determine whether they can continue to stay on the board and remain effective.		× 3 =	
6. The project meets a valid need. The completed project will fill a justifiable and urgent need, and has been tested in such a way that there is some substantiation. Further, the project helps fulfill your mission and is in keeping with your philosophy of operation. Give yourself a full "10" if it meets all these criteria.		× 3 =	
7. The case for the program has emotional and dramatic appeal. In order to raise important funds, a project must be compelling and have sizzle! Otherwise, no matter how valid the need, you won't raise funds. If you feel the case can be dramatized in such a way that it tugs at both the heart—and the purse-strings—give yourself a "10." If the sense of urgency and excitement is lacking, lower your score accordingly.		× 3 =	
8. On your board, you have a person of sufficient strength, stature, influence, and affluence that he or she will be a desirable candidate to head your campaign. However, it isn't necessary to choose your chair from the board roster (but this often makes the selection easier and certainly more natural). If you do have this caliber of person on your board, it also says something about the power of your group.		× 2 =	
9. The organization has successfully met its objective in its annual support campaign in the past two years. A group that cannot raise annual support will not be able to mount a major capital campaign. If you have gone over goal in the campaign, give yourself a "10." If you have just met goal, a "9." Anything less than that, begin decreasing your score accordingly. If you do not have an annual campaign for sustaining funds, give yourself a "1."		× 2 =	

(Continued)

EXERCISE 8.1   *(Continued)*

Factor	Score	Weight	Total
10. In the past two years, you've operated within a balanced budget. People give to organizations that are fiscally responsible and demonstrate proper financial stewardship. A balanced budget provides evidence of sound management and board accountability. Give yourself a "10" for a surplus and grade lower for an operating deficit.		× 2 =	
11. You have prepared a carefully developed pro-forma budget and have projected that when the facility is completed, the project will generate sufficient income to make it self-supporting. Raising funds for the ongoing operation of the project or for the programs that will take place in a new facility can sometimes be more difficult than raising funds for the capital campaign. Major credit goes to the operation that has a significant percentage of its budget that's self-supporting. If the project demonstrates it will generate significant income over expense, give yourself a "10." And congratulations! If the campaign includes funds for an endowment, increase your rating.		× 2 =	
12. A general rule of thumb is that you will be able to raise ten to fifteen times the funds in a capital campaign that you have been raising annually. Take the more liberal figure, fifteen, for instance. If your project needs more than fifteen times what you've been raising annually, you'll find it difficult to meet your objective. You're going to have to do better on your annual campaign. If the total capital project equals fifteen times your annual giving (or less), give yourself a "10." The higher the numerical ratio between your capital effort and your annual giving, the lower your rating.		× 2 =	
13. Beyond the 20 sources you identified in question 4, can you list the next 200 sources that are most likely to provide the largest gifts for your program? It's quite likely that these 220 sources will together give 80% to 90% of all the funds you receive. You need to determine now who these sources are. Your top leadership should be developed from these sources. This truly becomes the heart and spirit of your successful campaign.		× 2 =	
14. If you were unable to respond positively to question 8, is there someone who isn't on your board but would have sufficient strength, stature, influence, and affluence to chair your capital campaign? If you've been able to identify a person with the level of regard and esteem described, and the person has already accepted the responsibility, you get roaring applause, and a "10." Even if you haven't posed the question, but you feel fairly certain the man or		× 2 =	

Factor	Score	Weight	Total
woman of the caliber described will accept, give yourself a "10," and cross your fingers.			
15. You will be able to recruit sufficient volunteers to mount a successful campaign effort. While it's clear your largest gifts will determine the level of your success, you'll still require a broad base of giving to ensure a victory. You will need a well-trained, enthusiastic, and happy worker for every 5 to 8 prospects. Give yourself a full "10" if you will be able to recruit the workers you need.		× 2 =	
16. There should be no campaigns in your service area being planned for the same period which will cause a serious conflict. For your effort, you'll require all the dedication possible of volunteers, donors, and media coverage in order to win your effort. There are some campaigns, even of a major size, that won't interfere with yours—but if there are other organizations similar to yours in character and nature, this could cause a problem. If you don't anticipate a conflict, give yourself a "10."		× 2 =	
17. Your executive director has been on the staff for a minimum of 24 months. Grade this a "10" if the executive has been with you for at least 24 months. Deduct a point for every three months less than 24 months.		× 1 =	
18. Your board is up to the full complement of membership allowable in your bylaws. Grade this a "10" if you have no vacancies. For each vacancy, give yourself "1" less in rating. For instance, if you have two vacancies, give yourself an "8."		× 1 =	
19. Board attendance during the past 18 months has averaged 80% or more. Total all the board meetings you've had during the past 18 months and compute the attendance. If it's 80% or more, give yourself a "10." For every 5% less than 80%, deduct 1 rating point. For instance, if you had an average of 63% attendance, you should receive a "5." (Note: If your attendance averages less than 50% for regularly scheduled meetings, you are in serious trouble as far as the vitality and commitment of the board is concerned. You should probably not even be thinking about a campaign!)		× 1 =	
20. The organization has a challenging annual dollar objective in its annual campaign that forces it to stand on tiptoes to achieve its objectives. It's not enough to merely reach your annual campaign goal. Your objective must push you.		× 1 =	
SCORE			___

TABLE 8.6

Interpreting Your Score in Exercise 8.1

Score	Interpretation
299 or less	You're not ready—not nearly so. You need to spend time improving in the critical areas that will determine your ability to reach the goal.
300–399	You're close. You still have some work to do before you can be assured of success. Begin now to make the necessary changes.
400–449	You'll almost certainly have a successful campaign. Take time to correct the few deficiencies you have.
450–500	You're ready. What are you waiting for?

Special Events

Special events—dinners, cocktail receptions, golf games, concerts—can yield millions in revenue for well-organized charities. Smart nonprofits also design special events to serve other purposes: cultivate donors, improve public relations, and boost staff morale, to name a few. But if your organization *wants to make money from a special event,* focus on factors that increase your revenue and keep a lid on the costs. Then plan for ways to meet your other, nonmonetary goals.

Use Exercise 8.2, and you'll discover some of those elements that may make or break your event.

Once you've filled in Exercise 8.2, use the following process to score your answers:

1. If you answered no to any question, put a 0 in the far-right column, regardless of that factor's weight.

2. For any question you answered yes, write 1 in the far-right column—unless there's a weighting factor in the second column from the right. In that case, enter that number instead on the right.

A perfect score is 35 points. To interpret your score, consult Table 8.7.

Planned Giving

Gift planning, more commonly known as planned giving, has seized the attention of fundraisers everywhere. For some, it's the magic elixir—the ingredient in the fundraising mix that can justify all the time, effort, and

EXERCISE 8.2

Do Special Events Make Sense for You?

	Factor	Yes	No	Weight	Total
1.	The organization's leadership is personally committed to meeting a specific dollar goal.			× 5 =	
2.	Six months in advance of the event, you have written contracts for underwriters or sponsors to defray all the costs.			× 5 =	
3.	Two volunteer cochairs and most committee chairs are veterans of previous events.			× 3 =	
4.	All of the tables are sponsored or all of the tickets are sold four weeks before the event. All table or ticket sales at the event are pure profit.			× 3 =	
5.	Your leaders each buy ten tickets and six weeks before the event commit to sell ten to fifty tickets each.			× 3 =	
6.	You have a written contract (with a substitution clause for a star of equal or greater magnitude) with a celebrity who is popular in your market, who will not have performed in the area for at least six months, and who supports your mission.			× 3 =	
7.	Your organization has a tradition of doing a great event on the same date every year, and the date connects to your mission—such as Valentine's Day for the Heart Fund or Lincoln's birthday for hand-gun control.			× 3 =	
8.	Your organization has a list of donors who have attended or supported previous events.			× 3 =	
9.	The organization has strong visibility in your community or is widely recognized among those who might be interested in attending the event.			× 3 =	
10.	The date, place, and cochairs for next year's event are selected and will be announced at this year's event.			× 2 =	
11.	You have planned ways to meet other, nonmonetary goals from the event (for example, publicity, leadership development, membership sales, fellowship, and solidarity—and fun!).			× 2 =	
	SCORE				————

Source: *Reprinted with permission from Joan Flanagan, author of* Successful Fundraising.

money invested by a charity in recruiting, educating, and cultivating donors. After all, it doesn't take many $250,000 bequests to defray several years' expenditures on a quarterly newsletter or even a direct mail donor-acquisition program. And both fundraisers and donors are becoming more comfortable with the complexity of gift planning.

TABLE 8.7

Interpreting Your Score in Exercise 8.2

Score	Interpretation
0–15	Forget it. Don't waste your time. This event might accomplish lots of good things, but it's not likely to make any money for your organization.
16–25	This event might make money—or it might not. You're leaving a lot to chance.
26–34	You've probably got a winner on your hands, but there's still risk in this venture. Not all the bases are completely covered.
35	Really? Well, all we can say is that if this event doesn't make you a bundle, you ought to be ashamed of yourselves!

According to *Giving USA 2000*, bequests accounted for approximately 8.2 percent, or $15.61 billion, of the $190.16 billion estimated to have been contributed to nonprofit organizations in 1999 (the most recent year for which statistics were available). Bequest giving increased by nearly 15 percent over the previous year. Just thirty years ago, bequests were less $2 billion.[*]

Four out of every five planned gifts in the United States are charitable bequests in wills or living trusts. But the very biggest individual gifts come through other forms of gift planning: charitable remainder trusts, charitable lead trusts, charitable gift annuities, pooled income funds, and other creations of lawyers' and accountants' art.

Many nonprofit organizations don't have a prayer of raising significant sums through bequests and other forms of planned gifts. Other groups do receive planned gifts, but they won't make up a significant portion of the organization's income.

So how does your organization get onto this gravy train (assuming you're not already on board)? In fact, is planned giving even an appropriate fundraising option for you? Exercise 8.3 will help you determine your organization's planned giving potential.

To complete the exercise, place a check mark in the appropriate column on the right in answering each question. Use the spaces labeled "Action" to jot down notes about specific steps you can take to move your organization closer to readiness for planned giving.

It may be pointless to proceed with a sophisticated gift planning program unless you answered yes to all nine questions in Exercise 8.3. Nevertheless,

---

[*]Kaplan, A. E. (ed.). *The Annual Report on Philanthropy for the Year 1999*. Indianapolis, Ind.: AAFRC Trust for Philanthropy, 2000.

EXERCISE 8.3

Is Planned Giving Within Your Reach?

Question	Yes	No	Not Sure
1. Is your organization old enough and well enough established to inspire confidence that it will survive for decades to come? ACTION:			
2. Does your organization have a long-term mission that justifies a multigenerational perspective? ACTION:			
3. Will donors be likely to view the work your organization does as a legacy they wish to leave for future generations? ACTION:			
4. Does your organization have a reputation for integrity, frugality, and effectiveness? ACTION:			
5. Do you possess a large enough pool of individual donors who have made gifts for some time to your organization and from whom you might seek planned gifts? ACTION:			
6. Do you have in place a program of donor communications and cultivation through which planned giving may be readily promoted (for example, newsletters and donor briefings)? ACTION:			
7. Do you have available the necessary legal and accounting resources to ensure that questions from donors or their financial advisers can be promptly and accurately answered? ACTION:			

(Continued)

EXERCISE 8.3 *(Continued)*			
Question	**Yes**	**No**	**Not Sure**
8. If you hope to secure planned gifts in forms other than bequests, do you have the staff capabilities necessary to deal face-to-face with individual donors—to discuss and follow through on the inevitably unique aspects of each planned gift? ACTION:			
9. Does your organization view planned giving as a vehicle for donors to carry out their philanthropic intentions rather than solely as a means to gain individual financial advantage? ACTION:			

some of the weaknesses you might uncover can be corrected. For example, if you lack a large enough pool of individual donors, your organization can invest in acquiring donors—and years later launch a very successful planned giving program. Indeed, many nonprofits can anticipate receiving only charitable bequests, because those organizations can't invest the resources to solicit and manage complicated planned gifts. And if your donor communications and cultivation program is inadequate, you can bolster these activities by investing the necessary resources in such activities as donor newsletters, open houses, and selective donor briefings. As a result, sometimes a nonprofit organization that's ill suited for sophisticated gift planning today can still lay the groundwork for receiving truly big gifts in the future.

Direct Mail

Direct mail has long been the most cost-effective way for most nonprofit organizations to identify and acquire new donors. Research repeatedly confirms that the majority of first-time gifts to charity are made by mail. And because those donors are principally acquired by mail, it's usually most effective to inform, cultivate, and upgrade them by mail too.

Despite its great advantage, direct mail fundraising is costly and complex. It is a little like what democracy is sometimes called: the worst possible form of government, except when compared to all the others.

Now, let's be clear about what we mean by direct mail. Most nonprofit organizations, even those that claim *not* to have direct mail programs, communicate with, and even solicit, their donors by mail.

Some charities maintain continuing efforts to acquire new donors from outside lists (for example, members of other organizations, subscribers to suitable periodicals, or homeowners in selected neighborhoods). These organizations use direct mail in a systematic and strategic effort as an integral part of their development programs. First, as a way to recruit or acquire donors or members. Then, as a means to build lasting relationships with them.

Even when organizations use direct mail in a systematic fashion, they take some risk. Mailings may be poorly conceived or poorly executed, or unfortunate timing could undermine success. Even for those organizations that avoid making big mistakes, the cost of direct mail fundraising may be out of proportion to its potential yield for any number of possible reasons:

- There may not be a large enough number of people who agree your organization fills an important need, or it may be difficult to find or assemble mailing lists on which their names and addresses appear.

- People may agree the work you're doing is important but not care strongly enough to send money. Or the gifts they do send may be too small or infrequent to offset the costs of sending them mailings.

- The ever-fickle public may feel the need you're filling has passed or simply that it isn't urgent enough to require immediate support.

- Your constituency or market may be too small to support an ongoing program of donor acquisition.

Exercise 8.4 will help you determine whether your organization is ready to undertake a full-fledged direct mail fundraising program. And if you conclude that your organization isn't ready for a full-scale direct mail program, remember that *every* nonprofit uses the mail to communicate with and solicit its donors. Many of the methods employed in large-scale direct mail fundraising programs are indeed transferable to the efforts of small organizations.

To complete the exercise, place a check mark in the appropriate column on the right in answering each question. Use the spaces labeled "Action" for notes about specific steps you can take to prepare your organization for a direct mail program. All eight factors are essential for success in direct mail fundraising. However, if you're not sure how to answer the last two questions but you answered yes to all the rest, a test of your organization's direct mail potential may be wise. That will be especially true if your fundraising strategy requires either growth or broadening your donor base as a way to achieve stability.

EXERCISE 8.4

Should Your Organization Launch a Direct Mail Program?

Question	Yes	No	Not Sure
1. Do you have the necessary capital to invest in an initial test mailing and to expand and sustain the program if the test is successful?	☐	☐	☐

COMMENTS: It's possible for an organization to mount an initial test mailing for ten thousand dollars or even less, but that's usually not advisable. For a fair test—one that will yield statistically valid results—you'll need to mail at least thirty thousand letters with samples from half a dozen lists (fifty thousand letters or more and ten lists are usually far better). That's likely to cost twenty thousand dollars at a minimum. With professional assistance where it counts the most—on strategy, the creative work, and list selection—it's more realistic to think of mailing larger quantities and investing even more in the writing and design of your initial test mailing. And the capital for the test mailing is only the beginning. Usually, additional (and larger) infusions of capital are essential, or the program dies. Direct mail is capital intensive. Its hunger for cash never ends.

ACTION:

	Yes	No	Not Sure
2. Can you bear the risk of an unsuccessful test mailing?	☐	☐	☐

COMMENTS: Face it: the money you invest in an initial test mailing is risk capital. You can't count on getting back even a nickel. The odds are, of course, that you'll recover a significant portion of your investment in the test. Somewhere between one-third and two-thirds of your outlay for a test mailing will come back immediately in gifts sent in response to your test appeal. Very few organizations are able to launch direct mail test programs at breakeven or even turn a modest profit. Very few. So you can expect at best to receive even one-third to two-thirds of the investment.

ACTION:

	Yes	No	Not Sure
3. Can you effectively distinguish your organization from others serving the same constituency? Is there something dramatic or unique about your organization or its work?	☐	☐	☐

COMMENTS: Lots of worthy charities labor valiantly for years, performing valuable services for an appreciative public. Only those that can set themselves apart from the rest in some obvious way have a chance to derive significant amounts of net revenue from direct mail: perhaps through the personality or reputation of the chief executive or a key board member, perhaps through something unique in their programs or their results, or perhaps because they're the only organization of their type serving a particular region or constituency. There has to be something about the organization that will sustain public interest.

ACTION:

Question	Yes	No	Not Sure
4. Are your mission and strategy clear, so that your programs can be packaged for a wider public?	☐	☐	☐

COMMENTS: There's nothing deadlier than a direct mail campaign built around a little of this and a little of that. Your mission must sing out from the written materials. And what you ask of prospective supporters must be immediately apparent—at a glance—in every letter you send. (Are you asking them to join as members? To support a particular campaign? To sign a postcard to the governor? To send a gift of twenty-five dollars or more?)

ACTION:

Question	Yes	No	Not Sure
5. Does your organization have the track record, name recognition, prestige, or credentials necessary to establish your credibility?	☐	☐	☐

COMMENTS: Consider how crazy it is for people to send money through the mail to support organizations they may never have heard of before. Yet they do that every day of the year because the written materials are credible. They tell a story—in evocative words, images, and other symbols—that persuades readers to trust that the cause or institution does what it says. Unless readers find something familiar in the materials you send, they'll throw them away without a second glance. You need to convert readers into believers, and do so instantly, by referring to the names of leaders or supporters or the group's history of accomplishment. And that won't work unless something's there to begin with. This test of credibility also means that your mailing should avoid using a format or style that is too far out of sync with what other organizations are sending out in the mail. What you and your staff find avant-garde and intriguing, donors may find strange and suspicious.

ACTION:

Question	Yes	No	Not Sure
6. Do you have sufficient staff (or an outside firm) to ensure donors will get the service they need?	☐	☐	☐

COMMENTS: If you're not ready *before* you mail to take the next step—acknowledging and processing those gifts and then building the donor history database—you're not ready for direct mail. Even more important, if your organization isn't equipped to manage relationships with donors you recruit through the mail, there's no point bringing them in the door. Almost regardless of how big it is, the first gift means little. The true rewards come only with time, in the form of subsequent (and sometimes larger) gifts.

ACTION:

(Continued)

EXERCISE 8.4   *(Continued)*

Question	Yes	No	Not Sure
7. Are the issues involved in your work specific, compelling, and of concern to a broad public?	☐	☐	☐

COMMENTS: Some charities get all the breaks! They do things with unfailing public appeal—saving puppies and kittens, for example, or preserving the rainforest, helping cancer patients, or feeding starving children. But most nonprofits face a harder sell. For some, the challenge may be (or at least seem) insurmountable. The harsh reality is that not all issues or causes will "work" in direct mail. Whatever you ask donors to support must be urgent and easy to understand and have obvious, significant impact on people's lives. Otherwise, you'll be better off trying to coax out gifts face-to-face in a capital campaign or major gifts drive.

ACTION:

Question	Yes	No	Not Sure
8. Is your organization committed for the long haul? In other words, are you considering the long-term value of donors over many years, and are you prepared to do what it takes to cultivate and upgrade those donors?	☐	☐	☐

COMMENTS: Direct mail yields up its treasure only over the long run. It's rare for a charity to make a profit on its first efforts in the mail (prospecting or donor acquisition campaigns). Usually, the profits come only after one or more subsequent appeals or membership renewal mailings, as well as warm gift acknowledgments and plenty of information distributed in your organization's newsletter.

ACTION:

Telephone Fundraising

Many fundraising managers dismiss telephone fundraising out of hand because of personal bias or resistance from board members. If you're caught in this trap, you may be leaving a great deal of money on the table and forgoing other valuable benefits besides. Nonprofits that include the telephone as one of their fundraising tools learn more about their donors, foster increased donor loyalty, and enjoy rising revenues—a share of the billions raised every year through this fast-spreading fundraising method.

Although boards of directors and nonprofit staff tend to dislike telephone fundraising, it is a disservice to your donors not to consider this tactic. Many organizations find that 20 to 30 percent of their donors or members *prefer* the convenience of making gifts over the telephone.

Of course, there are some forms of telephone fundraising you may be wise to reject. Selling merchandise by telephone isn't likely to lay a firm foundation for a long-term philanthropic relationship. Nor is using unqualified callers to read mechanically from a script (even if the callers are volunteers).

It's also wise to tread cautiously into the fields of telephone prospecting. Acquiring new donors by telephone is most successful when you have access to telephone-responsive people: individuals who have made inquiries, actual donors, or prospects who may already have some relationship with your organization. For example, you may have some success in contacting prospects who have called your toll-free number for information to become members. But calling everyone in the telephone book is a waste of time for most nonprofits (and a nuisance, too, as far as we're concerned).

Finally, telephone fundraising is the most highly regulated of the fundraising methods. There are stiff penalties for those who fail to follow the regulations. More and more organizations are turning to professional telephone fundraising firms because, in addition to the results they achieve, those agencies can help groups make their way through the maze of state and federal restrictions that apply to telephone appeals.

Despite these complications, your organization can benefit from a program that employs the building blocks of professional telephone fundraising:

- Highly motivated callers
- Thorough training
- Careful supervision
- Precise selection of the target audience
- Scrupulous attention to fundraising ethics
- Compliance with all legal requirements, including registration with regulators of state charities

Exercise 8.5 outlines eight questions you can ask to determine whether professional telephone fundraising is right for your organization. A yes answer to any of these questions may be enough to justify the time and expense required to undertake a telephone fundraising program. You may use the "Action" spaces for notes about steps you can take to prepare for telephone fundraising.

Telephone fundraising is not a panacea for all that may ail your development program, but a great many nonprofits have found themselves in far

EXERCISE 8.5

Should Your Organization Use Telephone Fundraising?

Question	Yes	No	Not Sure
1. Does your organization have large numbers of lapsed or former donors?	☐	☐	☐

COMMENTS: If you answered yes, a telephone reinstatement program may be in order. Nonprofit organizations routinely discover that lapsed and former donors or members can be cost-effectively reactivated by telephone long after direct mail efforts cease to be worthwhile. And a far larger percentage of lapsed or former donors are likely to resume their support when contacted by telephone than will respond to even the most effective letter. Sometimes even long-lapsed donors—those whose most recent gift was received three or more years ago—can be reactivated by telephone at breakeven.

ACTION:

	Yes	No	Not Sure
2. Is your organization launching (or building) a monthly sustainer program?	☐	☐	☐

COMMENTS: Charities throughout the United States are turning to monthly giving programs to upgrade donors who aren't responsive to appeals for large lump-sum gifts. Time and again, calling them on the telephone has proven to be the most effective way to persuade such donors to take the big step of pledging monthly gifts, often through electronic funds transfer or preauthorized credit card charges. The target group typically includes both long-time donors of small, frequent gifts and new donors whose first gift was only recently received.

ACTION:

	Yes	No	Not Sure
3. Does your organization want to set up (or expand) a high-dollar or annual giving club?	☐	☐	☐

COMMENTS: A great many nonprofits identify prime prospects for major gifts by inviting their more generous direct mail–acquired donors or members to join giving clubs, usually starting at the $500 or $1,000 level. Telephone fundraising can be used, often in combination with specially tailored, upscale direct mail packages, to boost the recruitment effort. Because of its directness and potential for meaningful interaction, the telephone is one of the best ways to induce donors to upgrade dramatically.

ACTION:

Question	Yes	No	Not Sure
4. Is the response to your direct mail appeals declining?	☐	☐	☐

COMMENTS: A telephone fundraising campaign may bring new life to your donor development program and provide you with a wealth of unfiltered, up-to-the-minute feedback from your donors.

ACTION:

Question	Yes	No	Not Sure
5. Is your first-year donor renewal rate disappointing?	☐	☐	☐

COMMENTS: Many organizations have discovered their donors or members are more likely to renew their support if there is an increased investment in educating, cultivating—even pampering—those individuals. Some charities are systematically calling new donors or members simply to say, "Thank you." Often, useful information (such as e-mail addresses or special interests) can be gathered when making these telephone calls. The cumulative impact of such efforts may have a dramatic effect on your renewal rate.

ACTION:

Question	Yes	No	Not Sure
6. Does your organization appeal to its most active donors less often than six times annually?	☐	☐	☐

COMMENTS: Focus groups reveal that committed donors want and expect frequent contact with the organizations they support. Telephone calls to donors whose gifts are recent and frequent will help build relationships with them—while generating substantial net revenue. But take care: frequent telephone contact is not advisable with all donors. Only with those whose individual donor history reveals a level of interest that justifies the expense and that suggests the donor may be interested in receiving a higher volume of information.

ACTION:

Question	Yes	No	Not Sure
7. Is there an emergency, an expiring challenge grant, or some other looming deadline that requires your organization to raise substantial new sums?	☐	☐	☐

COMMENTS: The speed and immediacy of telephone contact make this tactic effective if quick turnaround is required to confront emergencies—and with deadlines of all other sorts. If there's time, the

(Continued)

EXERCISE 8.5   *(Continued)*

---

combination of direct mail and telephone contact, with one preceding the other by a few days or a couple of weeks, may be the best response to a fundraising challenge.

ACTION:

		Yes	No	Not Sure
8.	Are there at least five thousand persons who may be called?	☐	☐	☐

COMMENTS: After you've answered the first seven questions, you still need at least five thousand individuals who may be included in one or another specialized telephone fundraising program. Without that threshold number, your organization will find it isn't cost-effective either to hire a telephone fundraising consultant for on-site assistance or to out-source the campaign to a professional firm. (If the number of donors in your potential pool is smaller than five thousand, you may be able to obtain professional assistance in designing an in-house operation and training volunteers.)

ACTION:

---

better financial health through careful application of professional telephone fundraising techniques. If you're still in doubt that telephone fundraising is right for your organization, take another look at the eight questions in Exercise 8.5. You may be overlooking a fundraising tactic that is ideally suited to achieving your objectives and your primary and secondary fundraising strategy.

Selecting the Right Fundraising Techniques

The previous exercises should have helped you evaluate your organization's readiness to use any or all of the five major fundraising tactics. Now it's time to select one or more of these five tactics to achieve each of the specific objectives you've set. Answering the ten questions in Exercise 8.6 will help you determine what method or technique is most likely to help you reach the objectives you've set.

After you've completed these fairly detailed exercises, you may wish to go back and write two or three specific new initiatives or substantive changes you want to make for each of the broad areas of fundraising tactics we've encouraged you to review in this chapter.

EXERCISE 8.6

Choosing Fundraising Techniques to Achieve Specific Objectives

Objective (from Step 7): _____

	Yes	No	Not Sure
1. Does meeting this objective require major gifts?	☐	☐	☐

If yes, then you should definitely consider a *capital campaign*. If you have some lead time, you may also find that *special events* can be a useful way to cultivate major donors. A specialized *telephone* campaign may be effective in securing major gifts as well. But typically, the best source of really big gifts is *planned giving*. Despite the name, your organization can't plan on when those gifts will be received.

	Yes	No	Not Sure
2. Can this objective be achieved over several years, and thus would multiyear commitments make sense?	☐	☐	☐

A *capital campaign* could be effective because you seek pledges or commitments that donors fulfill over three to five years.

	Yes	No	Not Sure
3. Does this objective involve increasing the number of donors?	☐	☐	☐

If yes, then *direct mail* is the fastest and most effective way to add new donors to your base of support. *Special events* can also attract a number of donors, but this may not be a stable source of income since those who attend a special event are less likely to make subsequent gifts.

	Yes	No	Not Sure
4. Would opportunities for involvement or recognition help achieve this objective—or simply get in the way?	☐	☐	☐

Capital campaigns and *special events* provide lots of opportunities for involvement and recognition. In the case of *planned giving,* a legacy society offers recognition or an opportunity to make gifts in memory of a loved one. Some sophisticated *direct mail* programs can offer simple recognition or even include involvement devices (surveys and petitions, for example), but generally direct mail and telephone fundraising work best if donors aren't too directly involved.

	Yes	No	Not Sure
5. Do you need publicity or public awareness to meet this objective?	☐	☐	☐

Successful *special events* can generate lots of publicity—and, conversely, they work best when you get good publicity. Response to your *direct mail* and *telephone* fundraising programs will be higher if your organization is well known in the community and in the media.

	Yes	No	Not Sure
6. Will this project be volunteer driven, or will the staff be almost totally responsible for carrying out this objective?	☐	☐	☐

If you don't have lots of volunteers, pass by *special events* and *capital campaigns*. *Direct mail, telephone,* and *planned giving* can all operate effectively with only staff.

(Continued)

EXERCISE 8.6   *(Continued)*

	Yes	No	Not Sure
7. Do you have a sense of the age of your donors? Do you have a sizable group of supporters who are over sixty years of age? Over seventy years of age? Has your organization been around for fifteen or twenty years?	☐	☐	☐

If yes, you may want to go back to Exercise 8.3 and see whether you can improve your organization's readiness for *planned giving*. And your *direct mail* program may be an effective way to achieve your specific objective, since older people are generally more responsive to direct mail than younger people.

	Yes	No	Not Sure
8. Do you know the state regulations that may apply to your fundraising activities? Do you have the staff or outside resources to ensure compliance with any regulatory obligations?	☐	☐	☐

If yes, you can proceed with *direct mail* and *telephone* fundraising. If no, you may want to achieve your objective through *special events* or perhaps a *capital campaign* that focuses on local donors.

	Yes	No	Not Sure
9. Do you have the staff and procedures in place or a suitable outsourcing arrangement to receive, record, and acknowledge a significant number of contributions?	☐	☐	☐

Direct mail and *telephone fundraising* require lots of gift processing.

	Yes	No	Not Sure
10. Does your organization have financial capital or resources to invest in achieving this objective?	☐	☐	☐

If yes, then you can use *direct mail* to meet your objective. A *special event* can require some financial risk taking. *Telephone* fundraising can be accomplished with a relative small investment, and a modest *capital campaign* can be undertaken at least at the outset with the sweat equity of your staff and board members.

Conclusion

Now that you've completed Step Eight, you might think you've reached the finish line. Not so. As helpful as it is to have selected the right methods and tactics to meet your objectives, you still have to put them to work if you're to succeed. The reality of organizational life, and sensitivity to your donors and funders, requires that you determine *when* you're going to make use of these fundraising tactics. In Step Nine, we show you how to create a master calendar that will help you use the right tactic at the right time.

Step Nine

Create a Master Calendar and Keep on Track

CONGRATULATIONS! You've chosen the best fundraising strategy for your organization, and you've identified a second strategy that will help move you in the direction you want to go. You've also done the hard work of coming up with ambitious goals, achievable objectives, and the specific tactics that will help you reach those goals and objectives.

But all this becomes useless theory and idle discussion unless there's a schedule that says when you will use the tactics you've chosen to meet your objectives. All too often, organizations fall short of their revenue goals because they don't devote enough time to fundraising activities. Other events and efforts get the staff and volunteers' attention, and before you know it, it's the last quarter of the year, and there isn't enough time left to reach all donors.

So how do you make sure you set aside enough time to meet your objectives? What factors should you consider when scheduling your development activities? Exercise 9.1 will help you zero in on the most important factors.

This is not an exercise for the entire strategy team. A responsible staff person or a very dedicated volunteer will need to set aside several hours (and for larger organizations, an entire day) to complete this exercise. However, even if this task has been delegated to someone else, you will benefit from reading the introductions to each part of the exercise. You'll find helpful reminders about how specific fundraising tactics or methods support your primary strategy.

When you complete Exercise 9.1, you'll realize you have a lot of work to do. (Actually, you already knew that, didn't you?) Now you have a better idea, though, of what follow-up action will help you achieve the objectives that will move you closer toward the goals you've set as part of your fundraising strategy.

EXERCISE 9.1

Factors in Scheduling Fundraising Activities

1. Have you scheduled opportunities (visits, telephone calls, or letters) to request gifts when donors are most responsive? Those times are December and January and, more generally, the last and first quarters of the year. Organizations that are pursuing an Efficiency strategy must make an especially intense effort to make the most of this giving season.

Follow-Up Actions for Your Organization

Task(s)	Responsible Person	Deadline
a. _____	_____	_____
b. _____	_____	_____
c. _____	_____	_____
d. _____	_____	_____

2. Are there at least some development activities and opportunities to give in every month of the year? You can never tell for certain when the interests and capacities of donors will intersect. Fundraising can't take a summer vacation! Especially if your strategy seeks Involvement, you have to schedule lots of different opportunities at different times of the year.

Follow-Up Actions for Your Organization

Task(s)	Responsible Person	Deadline
a. _____	_____	_____
b. _____	_____	_____
c. _____	_____	_____
d. _____	_____	_____

3. Successful fundraising campaigns allow ample time for planning. For example, if your organization is contemplating a capital campaign, have you scheduled a feasibility study or precampaign assessment, a board meeting devoted to reviewing the study and formally authorizing the campaign, and a campaign announcement activity after you've secured the necessary lead gifts? Capital campaigns are probably the most effective tools in an Efficiency strategy. They can also increase Visibility and usually require lots of Involvement.

Follow-Up Actions for Your Organization

Task(s)	Responsible Person	Deadline
a. _____	_____	_____
b. _____	_____	_____
c. _____	_____	_____
d. _____	_____	_____

4. Will each donor receive at least four issues of a newsletter, spread out somewhat evenly throughout the year? Many donors feel that information is the greatest benefit of their financial support and the strongest motivation to keep giving. Newsletters can also build excitement and enthusiasm if your strategy is Growth. And newsletters need to be part of a multifaceted public relations campaign if your strategy is Visibility.

    Follow-Up Actions for Your Organization

Task(s)	Responsible Person	Deadline
a. _____	_____	_____
b. _____	_____	_____
c. _____	_____	_____
d. _____	_____	_____

5. When will you publish your organization's annual report? For those organizations seeking Stability, accountability is essential to your organization's ethical conduct, and making your financial statements available to your donors helps position your organization as trustworthy. Sending an annual report to at least your more generous donors is also an excellent way to implement a strategy of Involvement.

    Follow-Up Actions for Your Organization

Task(s)	Responsible Person	Deadline
a. _____	_____	_____
b. _____	_____	_____
c. _____	_____	_____
d. _____	_____	_____

6. Will the appropriate age group of donors hear at least twice a year about the benefits of charitable bequests and other planned gifts? The biggest checks an organization is likely to receive are from individuals who wish to leave a legacy of financial support. Nonprofits looking for Stability should schedule even more planned giving cultivation mailings and activities.

    Follow-Up Actions for Your Organization

Task(s)	Responsible Person	Deadline
a. _____	_____	_____
b. _____	_____	_____
c. _____	_____	_____
d. _____	_____	_____

(Continued)

EXERCISE 9.1   *(Continued)*

7. At least once a year, will a significant group of donors be invited to begin making monthly gifts using a credit card or electronic funds transfer? Will others be asked to make their annual gift or renew their membership? Will letters or telephone calls remind those who haven't given yet? If your strategy is Efficiency or Stability, keeping up a steady flow of gifts is essential.

    Follow-Up Actions for Your Organization

Task(s)	Responsible Person	Deadline
a. _____	_____	_____
b. _____	_____	_____
c. _____	_____	_____
d. _____	_____	_____

8. Will there be at least one event a year that expresses thanks and recognition to your donors (a dinner, luncheon, lecture, or party, for example)? This is not a fundraising event but rather something you do to honor those whose support sustains your organization. Very few of your donors will attend, but they will appreciate the invitation. These donor events are also a great opportunity for Involvement and Visibility.

    Follow-Up Actions for Your Organization

Task(s)	Responsible Person	Deadline
a. _____	_____	_____
b. _____	_____	_____
c. _____	_____	_____
d. _____	_____	_____

9. Did you schedule at least one mailing, telephone program, event, or campaign to recruit new donors? No matter what your primary strategy is, you must plan for some level of growth, because donor attrition is inevitable. A Growth strategy requires you to schedule several efforts throughout the year to acquire new donors.

    Follow-Up Actions for Your Organization

Task(s)	Responsible Person	Deadline
a. _____	_____	_____
b. _____	_____	_____
c. _____	_____	_____
d. _____	_____	_____

10. You may want to consider scheduling one or more of the following events or activities:

- At least three months before the end of your fiscal year, a session to plan next year's development activities
- At least six cultivation or informational mailings to your most generous ten to one hundred donors or prospects
- Presentation of the development plan to the board of directors
- A luncheon or other activity to thank volunteers (and staff) who've been involved in implementing your organization's fundraising strategy
- Deadlines for submitting grants
- Completion of reports required by grants
- Site visits by grantors and potential grantors
- Annual or semiannual analysis of donor database
- Completion of IRS 990 form and posting on the Web, a form that the Internal Revenue Service requires most nonprofits to file and that many state regulating agencies also review before accepting an organization's registration in that state
- Renewal of registrations as required by the appropriate state charities office or attorney general
- An annual fundraising event or events (If you have more than three major events a year and your fundraising strategy isn't Visibility, go back through this workbook and double-check your fundraising strategy!)

Follow-Up Actions for Your Organization

Task(s)	Responsible Person	Deadline
a. _____	_____	_____
b. _____	_____	_____
c. _____	_____	_____
d. _____	_____	_____

Fortunately, you don't have to do all this work tomorrow. Choosing the right strategy helps you stay focused on your long-term priorities so you can spread out the work over time. Exercise 9.2 will help you assign specific months and weeks to the follow-up actions you identified in Exercise 9.1. We've sketched a sample master calendar for the first two months, which appears as Table 9.1. We've broken each month into weeks, a step that you'll probably want to do, sooner or later.

Exercise 9.2 contains seven unlabeled columns, each of which is to represent one fundraising track or tactic (such as major gifts, planned giving, or direct mail). You may label these tracks as you wish, corresponding to the tactics or fundraising programs that your organization uses. You may wish to add more columns, and probably should do so if your organization

TABLE 9.1

Sample Master Calendar for Fundraising Success

	Major Donors or Capital Campaign	Promotion of Charitable Bequests and Planned Gifts	Special Events	Direct Mail and Membership	Telephone Fundraising
January, Week 1				Winter newsletter	
January, Week 2	Cultivation mailing		Save-the-date postcard for dinner		
January, Week 3		Legacy society invitation		Annual renewal mailing	
January, Week 4	Visit donors in Minneapolis				
February, Week 1					Recruit new monthly donors
February, Week 2			Catering arrangements for dinner		
February, Week 3	Select firm to conduct feasibility study	Update listing of Legacy Society		Second notice for annual renewal	
February, Week 4		Legacy Society luncheon	Recruit master of ceremonies		
March, Week 1	Visit donors in Chicago				Invite lapsed donors to reactivate

is large and complex. The CD-ROM at the back of this workbook will allow you to add columns to enlarge the master calendar.

The left-hand column notes the months of the year. Use the cells to the right of each month to log in any necessary activity for each track in turn: for example, "donor renewal mailing," "major donor visits," "estate planning seminar," "annual banquet." You may have to leave blank spaces, perhaps even a lot of them. But don't worry. Use only the spaces you need

EXERCISE 9.2

Creating Your Master Calendar for Fundraising

Fundraising Tactic, Method, or Program

Month						
January						
February						
March						
April						
May						
June						
July						
August						
September						
October						
November						
December						

to use to describe the principal activities required to help you reach your objectives (and, ultimately, your goals).

Once you've completed filling in the master calendar form, you may determine that you've bunched too many activities together into one month or one season. Review your choices, and make timing adjustments as good judgment requires—for example, moving a mailing from one month to the next, advancing the schedule for your major donor visits, or whatever else it takes to smooth out your work flow and operate within the cash flow limitations imposed by your organization's finances.

Success in fundraising, as in so many other realms of human activity, lies in attention to detail. Once you've completed your twelve-month master fundraising calendar, you may find it advantageous to flesh out the first two or three months with the level of detail permitted by a week-by-week calendar and to repeat that exercise every two to three months. But that will take you deep into the province of execution.

Conclusion

It's now time to leave the world of strategic planning for a while and immerse yourself once again in the real world of day-to-day fundraising. The hard work starts now—and so does the pleasure that comes with sustained fundraising success.

There is, though, one more step you can take to increase the likelihood that all your hard work will fulfill your fundraising strategy. As you put this book down to get busy implementing your plans, you'll want to mark your calendar now to be sure that at least every six months, you turn to Step Ten. Here in this final step, you'll find some exercises and suggestions to help you monitor progress and make adjustments that will keep you on your strategic course.

Step Ten

Measure Your Organization's Progress

THERE'S AN OLD saying to the effect that if you're headed nowhere in particular, you'll likely end up there. In your case, though, you *are* headed someplace very particular: you and your strategy team have chosen a primary and a secondary strategy to give direction to your organization's fundraising efforts. You've also articulated some ambitious goals, set specific objectives, and selected tactics or methods to carry out those objectives.

And we hope you've followed our advice and made your objectives ones that can be measured. Indeed, it's this ability to be measured—to be evaluated or reviewed in a quantifiable way—that makes this strategic approach to fundraising such a powerful tool in fulfilling your organization's larger mission.

By its very nature, every one of the objectives you've set is quantifiable and can thus be viewed as a benchmark. You can measure your progress toward these benchmarks as often as makes good sense—and it's essential that you do so. As the months go by, you'll find you're making more progress in some areas than in others, so you'll either want to adjust the allocation of your resources to give more emphasis to your efforts in areas where you're lagging or revise the objectives you've set. It may be that your objectives were unrealistic or perhaps even unneeded to meet your goal.

Aside from the unforeseen and unpredictable nature of carrying out objectives, there are other factors that can complicate the pursuit of your organization's fundraising strategy:

- Fundraising is a continuous, long-term process—a process of building strong relationships with donors—and there's rarely a time when the process is complete. By working your way through this manual, you've made use of a set of tools to reassess and realign your resource development program. Implementing your new strategy and tactics will take years.

- As time goes on, some tactics will work, and others won't. It's vital that you keep tabs on the performance of each element in your fundraising program, dropping those that prove unsuccessful and either adopting new techniques or investing more heavily in those that prove to work as expected.

- Conditions change over time. The economy waxes and wanes. Key staff members come and go. There are demographic shifts, changes in public taste and mood, and new developments in technology. All of this means that you—and your fundraising program—can't stand still.

That's why it's important to set aside time at least every six months to examine your efforts systematically. In organizations with more complex development programs and with multiple staff responsible for those programs, quarterly or even monthly review is advised. Regular review of your fundraising efforts opens up the possibility of introducing a midcourse correction if needed. Ideally, given the dynamic nature of fundraising, you'll establish a discipline of continuous evaluation. Step Ten will introduce you to several assessment tools that will help you through that process.

We encourage you to assemble many, if not all, of the members of your original strategy team. By following the two exercises in Step Ten, you will determine how far you've come and how much further you've got to go to achieve the organizational goals you've set.

We suggest that you avoid spending too much time on this process of assessment. If you're meeting in a group, plan on two to three hours. Don't get trapped into seeking precise measurements or answering every question in great detail. Some groups spend so much time keeping track of their progress and second-guessing their activities that they don't get around to meeting with donors and asking for gifts. In most cases, getting an overall sense of how your organization is doing will do the most to inspire you and others to improve your efforts in the future.

Begin with Exercise 10.1, which will allow you to assess your progress toward your fundraising objectives. Copy each objective from the fundraising strategic plan you drafted in Step Seven into columns 1 and 2. In column 3, write down the number that represents what you have actually achieved in your work toward each of those objectives. Column 4 will show the variance in absolute numbers and column 5 the difference in percentage terms.

EXERCISE 10.1

Measuring Progress Toward Your Objectives

Objective (from Step 7)	Target[a]	Actual	Difference	Percentage Difference
GOAL 1				
a. _____	_____	_____	_____	_____
b. _____	_____	_____	_____	_____
c. _____	_____	_____	_____	_____
GOAL 2				
a. _____	_____	_____	_____	_____
b. _____	_____	_____	_____	_____
c. _____	_____	_____	_____	_____
GOAL 3				
a. _____	_____	_____	_____	_____
b. _____	_____	_____	_____	_____
c. _____	_____	_____	_____	_____
GOAL 4				
a. _____	_____	_____	_____	_____
b. _____	_____	_____	_____	_____
c. _____	_____	_____	_____	_____
GOAL 5				
a. _____	_____	_____	_____	_____
b. _____	_____	_____	_____	_____
c. _____	_____	_____	_____	_____

[a]*Refers to the measurable or quantifiable dimension of your objective—for example, "Recruit 100 new monthly sustainers by December 31."*

Note that we've allowed space in the exercise for up to five goals and with up to three objectives corresponding to each of those goals. Use the CD-ROM to add lines if you have more than three objectives for each goal. But remember, if you have too many objectives for one goal, it may actually be two goals.

When you've completed Exercise 10.1, you'll have discovered several instances where you haven't come close to meeting your objective (the percentage is 75 percent or lower). For those objectives, we recommend that you take time to estimate your organization's investment in those objectives in the three key categories:

- Number of staff assigned

- Number of staff or volunteer hours

- Budget allocated to meeting this objective

For objectives where there's a significant difference between the target and the actual, we also urge you to take note of two other factors:

- Specific changes in external environment

- Unforeseen circumstances or developments that occurred since the time you originally set your objectives

By taking time to review those objectives where you fell short, you'll learn whether the objective itself was inappropriate or whether the execution was faulty.

After you've determined how close or how far you are toward achieving the individual objectives you and your team have set, you'll next want to assess your progress toward the broader goals that encompass those objectives.

Turn to Exercise 10.2, and copy into the spaces indicated the goals you set in Step Six. Ask each member of the strategy team to jot down in the next column on his or her own copy of Exercise 10.2 a personal assessment of the organization's progress toward each goal, with ideas for corrective action, if any, in the last column. Then, informed by a review of the picture you painted with Exercise 10.1, share your views in a group discussion, and strive for consensus. In full view of all the facts, consensus on how far you've gone may be easy to achieve. Agreement on corrective action might be more elusive—but that's what discussion and teamwork are for!

For an additional check on your progress, complete Exercise 10.3. For each of the five strategies, we've identified a single strategic benchmark that comes as close as we can find to a one-size-fits-all measurement of progress (except for Involvement, where two interrelated benchmarks seem important). We suggest you fill out two rows on this form: one for your primary

EXERCISE 10.2

Measuring Progress Toward Your Goals

Goal 1: _____

Progress:

Corrective Action:

Goal 2: _____

Progress:

Corrective Action:

Goal 3: _____

Progress:

Corrective Action:

Goal 4: _____

Progress:

Corrective Action:

Goal 5: _____

Progress:

Corrective Action:

EXERCISE 10.3

Reviewing Your Strategic Benchmarks

Strategy	Benchmark	Number Six Months Ago	Number Today	Difference
Growth	Number of active donors			
Involvement	Number of activities for donors			
	Number of donors who participate			
Visibility	Number of media citations[a]			
Efficiency	Cost to raise a dollar			
Stability	Number of fundraising programs that yield 15 percent or more of total revenue[b]			

[a]*Over previous six-month period. Includes newspapers, magazines, books, radio, television, and the Internet.*

[b]*Takes into account all private voluntary contributions to revenue, including major gifts, planned gifts, foundation grants, corporate gifts, membership, ticket revenue, merchandising, and other major sources of financial support.*

strategy and the other for your secondary one. Insert in the proper spaces the number that represents that benchmark six months ago (or three months ago if you review your results on a quarterly basis or twelve months ago for an annual review) and today's corresponding number. The final column provides space for you to calculate the difference.

Exercise 10.3 is not a rigorous scientific check, but the differences between today and six months ago should point to the progress you're making—or highlight the lack of it.

At this point, either in your own private review or as part of the group discussion, you may want to list circumstances that contributed to your organization's either meeting its strategic benchmark or falling short. Especially if you've missed the mark, you'll want to look again at your work in Steps Seven and Eight to make sure that your objectives were realistic and that you selected fundraising tactics appropriate to carrying out those objectives.

Objectives, Goals, and Benchmarks May Not Be Enough

We hope this workbook has helped your organization discover the best strategy for success in fundraising and that we've given you a big head start on executing the goals and objectives that will help you fulfill the strategy you've chosen. Before you finish your evaluation of your progress in this important endeavor, we urge you to measure one additional facet of your work.

One of the benefits of carrying out the strategic planning process we've outlined is that your organization's communications in newsletters and other publications and with the media will become more effective. Clarity about your strategy will lead to greater clarity in your organization's message.

Yet an organization's fundraising efforts often fail not because of an unfocused strategy or even because of faulty execution. Rather, the message as presented, especially in written materials, is mishandled. In other words, the way you communicate with your donors and funders, as well as with your staff, board, and volunteers, fails to reflect the full import of your strategic direction.

That's why we encourage you to complete Exercise 10.4, which will help you assess whether you're getting your organization's message across with your written materials. First, assemble a generous collection of the most recently printed brochures, flyers, press releases, solicitations, proposals, and reports. Then review these materials in the light of the eight criteria. Then assign an overall rating in response to each of the eight questions, with 5 being best and 0 the worst. Once you've covered all eight criteria, multiply the score you've assigned on each row by the weight assigned, and write the product of those two numbers in the last column 5. Finally, total the numbers in the last column.

With as many as five points available for each of the eight criteria, and weighting factors that total 24, a perfect score is 120 points. You may translate a numerical score into a letter grade by consulting Table 10.1.

As a final step in gaining perspective on the progress you've made since you set out to pursue a new fundraising strategy, we suggest that you complete Exercise 10.5. This is the same as Exercise 1.1, which you completed in Step One at the beginning of this process. By contrasting your answers to these ten questions a year after embarking on a new course for your organization, you'll get a sense of whether the work you're doing is truly having the strategic impact you want to achieve.

As you and your strategy team share your responses to Exercise 10.5, you may want to articulate specific ways that having primary and secondary strategies has improved your ability to respond positively to the ten questions. Responding to these questions may also lead you to identify

EXERCISE 10.4

Is Your Message Getting Through?

	Criterion	Score	Weight	Total
1.	Does every piece of written material—every brochure, flyer, press release, solicitation, proposal, and report—prominently and consistently display the elements of your organizational identity (logo, tagline if any, plus any distinctive colors or typeface)?		× 5 =	
2.	Does every piece of written material—every brochure, flyer, press release, solicitation, proposal, and report—clearly reflect your organization's positioning—that is, does it emphasize your organizational vision and your unique purpose or accomplishments?		× 5 =	
3.	Is the writing in your materials consistently clear, so that even a casual reader will understand the gist of your message and careful readers will not become bogged down in ambiguities?		× 3 =	
4.	Are the messages you deliver through your written materials honest and accurate? Or do they make you uncomfortable because they exaggerate your organization's strengths or accomplishments?		× 3 =	
5.	Does every message you deliver to individual donors or members or to prospective supporters highlight the benefits of supporting your cause, not just your needs as an organization?		× 3 =	
6.	Do all of your written materials feature a powerful writing style? This means using the shortest possible words, short sentences, and short paragraphs, and an absolute minimum of technical jargon, foreign expressions, abbreviations, and acronyms.		× 2 =	
7.	Are your materials formatted and designed for easy reading, using adequate type size, generous margins, clear indentations, bullets, underlining, and other devices to assist the reader?		× 2 =	
8.	Do your written materials effectively use color, graphics, and white space to emphasize the essential elements of your message?		× 1 =	
	SCORE			_____

TABLE 10.1

Interpreting Your Score in Exercise 10.4

Rating	Letter Grade	Meaning
110–120	A+	No more need be said.
100–109	A	Give that writer a pat on the back!
80–99	B	Shows lots of promise.
60–79	C	Needs some improvement.
30–59	D	Requires a lot of work. Maybe better to start from scratch!
0–29	F	Uh oh!

EXERCISE 10.5

Ten Questions Every Nonprofit Board Member or Executive Needs to Answer

Question	Yes	No	Not Sure	Weight	Score
1. Are you raising more money every year?				× 3 =	
2. Does your funding come from several different sources, activities, or techniques, with no single source accounting for 60 percent or more? (Typical *sources* are foundations, corporations, special events, and the annual fund. Typical *techniques* are direct mail or planned giving.)				× 3 =	
3. Do you always have enough cash to pay your bills, plus a reserve fund to allow for contingencies?				× 3 =	
4. Does every member of your board without exception contribute money at least once a year?				× 3 =	
5. Is one senior-level person clearly designated as responsible for planning and monitoring your fundraising efforts?				× 3 =	
6. Are your financial resources scaled to match your organization's goals? In other words, can you honestly say your resources are adequate to match the scope of your ambitions, so that you're not greatly underfunded—or, conversely, that you don't command resources far in excess of what you require to accomplish your mission so that your organization is overfunded?				× 3 =	
7. Are you raising money from reliable, predictable sources, such as endowment income, membership dues, or monthly sustainer gifts, to cover your fixed expenses (that is, your overhead)? And if it's necessary, are you funding only variable expenses from less predictable sources, such as foundation grants, major gifts, or income from special appeals?				× 3 =	
8. Are your organization's fundraising activities scheduled in advance and carried out on time?				× 3 =	
9. Is your record-keeping system efficient and accurate?					
• Do you know how, where, and by whom your donor giving records are maintained, and what information is on file?				× 1 =	
• Do thank-you letters to your donors go out within seventy-two hours of the receipt of the gift and the same day for those who make major gifts?				× 1 =	
• Do you have the names and telephone numbers of your top ten or twenty donors at your fingertips?				× 1 =	
10. Does your organization have clearly understood policies on fundraising ethics, preferably in writing?				× 3 =	
Number answered "Not Sure"					
SCORE					

one or more areas where you'd like to review your fundraising goals, objectives, and tactics to make sure they are truly contributing to your strategic success.

And if completing these five exercises has surfaced lots of shortcomings and other problems, you would be well advised to revisit the primary strategy you selected. Every organization makes mistakes and encounters unforeseen problems in implementing a new strategy. But if difficulties abound, that may be an indication that you picked the wrong strategy—at least for your organization at this point in its history.

Congratulations!

However your measurement exercises turn out in Step Ten, you deserve to be congratulated. The new insights from this evaluation process will help you devise any corrective steps you need to take or to gain new energy from the continuing work ahead. And by taking the time and having the courage to measure your progress, you'll be much more likely next year to have traveled even farther down the road toward your strategic goal. Over the years, you'll come to look forward to measuring your ever greater success.

It may take months or even years to see the real payoff for all the time, effort, and talent you've invested in developing your fundraising strategy. But if you stick to your strategy, pursue your goals single-mindedly, and carefully monitor your progress on a continuing basis, making course corrections as they become necessary, you *will* succeed. You will succeed because the progress of your fundraising programs and your development projects will bring your organization closer to fulfilling its mission.

We wish you the very best in all your fundraising endeavors!

Glossary of Key Terms

Fundraising strategy The primary direction of your resource development program; the way your organization proposes to use fundraising techniques to marshal the financial resources you need and support your organizational strategy. A true fundraising strategy encompasses the financial development priorities (as distinct from goals) that your organization has set. Typically, a fundraising strategy remains in place for a minimum of three to five years but must be reassessed at least that frequently.

Goals The chief components of strategy. Goals are often devilishly vague or imprecise. They're ambitious, frequently almost unattainable targets that move your organization closer to the strategic end you've adopted. Goals are seldom achieved within any one year.

Master calendar A schedule of activities or programs that an organization uses to put fundraising tactics to work. It enables an organization to spread those activities and programs over the weeks and months of a twelve-month period.

Mission The overarching purpose that is the reason your organization continues to operate. Often this larger purpose is articulated in a mission statement, which we believe should be less than a page (and, ideally, no more than three or four sentences). The mission typically defines the audience you seek to serve, the way in which you serve them, and the results you are striving to achieve.

Objectives Precise targets that can be measured and are achievable within a specific time period (typically a year or less). Goals are realized in part as an organization achieves objectives.

Strategic plan Typically a written document that articulates an organization's mission and outlines the primary strategy it will follow to pursue that mission over the next three to five years. Often it reflects a systematic assessment of the organization's strengths and weaknesses, as well as the opportunities and threats the organization faces as it seeks to carry out its mission. Ideally, this plan includes the major goals and specific objectives that will enable your organization to achieve its strategic ends.

Strategy The primary direction your organization is taking; the way it proposes to change itself and affect the public you seek to serve. A true organizational strategy encompasses the priorities (as distinct from goals) that your organization has set, including those that point the way toward your programmatic goals and those that represent the means you choose to pursue those goals. Typically, an organizational strategy remains in place for a minimum of three to five years but must be reassessed at least that frequently.

Strategy team A committee or task force ideally with at least five individuals but no more than twelve persons who have a variety of perspectives and responsibilities. This strategy planning team meets for three to six sessions to follow a process that selects a strategy and sets major goals.

Tactics Tools, methods, techniques, or activities that are used to help an organization achieve its objectives. In fundraising, tactics often correspond to the channels or sources from which an organization receives contributed funds. There are dozens of proven tactics (also called fundraising techniques), but five are widely used and serve as a foundation for other fundraising tactics: a capital or major donor campaign, special events, planned giving, direct mail, and telephone fundraising.

How to Use the CD-ROM

System Requirements

Windows PC

- 486 or Pentium processor-based personal computer
- Microsoft Windows 95 or Windows NT 3.51 or later
- Minimum RAM: 8 MB for Windows 95 and NT
- Available space on hard disk: 8 MB Windows 95 and NT
- 2X speed CD-ROM drive or faster
- Netscape 4.0 or higher browser or MS Internet Explorer 4.0 or higher

Macintosh

- Macintosh with a 68020 or higher processor or Power Macintosh
- Apple OS version 7.0 or later
- Minimum RAM: 12 MB for Macintosh
- Available space on hard disk: 6MB Macintosh
- 2X speed CD-ROM drive or faster
- Netscape 4.0 or higher browser or MS Internet Explorer 4.0 or higher

NOTE: This CD requires Netscape 4.0 or MS Internet Explorer 4.0 or higher. It also uses the free Acrobat reader. You can download these products using the links below:

http://www.netscape.com/download/index.html
http://www.microsoft.com/windows/ie/download/default.asp
http://www.adobe.com/products/acrobat/readstep.html

Getting Started

Insert the CD-ROM into your drive. The CD-ROM will usually launch automatically. If it does not, click on the CD-ROM drive on your computer to launch. You will see an opening page. You can click on this page or wait for it to fade to the Copyright Page. After you click to agree to the terms of the Copyright Page, the Home Page will appear.

Moving Around

Use the buttons at the left of each screen or the underlined text at the bottom of each screen to move among the menu pages. To view a document listed on one of the menu pages, simply click on the name of the document. To quit a document at any time, click the box at the upper right-hand corner of the screen.

Use the scrollbar at the right of the screen to scroll up and down each page.

To quit the CD-ROM, you can click the Quit option at the bottom of each menu page, hit Control-Q, or click the box at the upper right-hand corner of the screen.

In Case of Trouble

If you experience difficulty using the *Ten Steps to Fundraising Success* CD-ROM, please follow these steps:

1. Make sure your hardware and systems configurations conform to the systems requirements noted under "Systems Requirements" above.

2. Review the installation procedure for your type of hardware and operating system. It is possible to reinstall the software if necessary.

3. You may call Jossey-Bass Customer Service at (415) 433-1740 between the hours of 8 A.M. and 5 P.M. Pacific Time, and ask for Jossey-Bass CD-ROM Technical Support.

Please have the following information available:

- Type of computer and operating system

- Version of Windows or Mac OS being used

- Any error messages displayed

- Complete description of the problem.

(It is best if you are sitting at your computer when making the call.)